THE CHALLENGE OF CHANGING YOUR LIFE

CLARA STELLA ARENAS
AND MIRNA PINEDA

BALBOA.
PRESS
A DIVISION OF HAY HOUSE

Balboa Press books may be ordered through booksellers or by contacting:

Balboa Press
A Division of Hay House
1663 Liberty Drive
Bloomington, IN 47403
www.balboapress.com
1 (877) 407-4847

Because of the dynamic nature of the Internet, any web addresses or links contained in this book may have changed since publication and may no longer be valid. The views expressed in this work are solely those of the author and do not necessarily reflect the views of the publisher, and the publisher hereby disclaims any responsibility for them.

The author of this book does not dispense medical advice or prescribe the use of any technique as a form of treatment for physical, emotional, or medical problems without the advice of a physician, either directly or indirectly. The intent of the author is only to offer information of a general nature to help you in your quest for emotional and spiritual well-being. In the event you use any of the information in this book for yourself, which is your constitutional right, the author and the publisher assume no responsibility for your actions.

Any people depicted in stock imagery provided by Thinkstock are models, and such images are being used for illustrative purposes only.
Certain stock imagery © Thinkstock.

Print information available on the last page.

ISBN: 978-1-5043-6423-2 (sc)
ISBN: 978-1-5043-6424-9 (hc)
ISBN: 978-1-5043-6438-6 (e)

Library of Congress Control Number: 2016913133

Balboa Press rev. date: 09/01/2016

DEDICATION

To each one of those who accepted the challenge of changing YOUR LIFE and who had confidence in the work that we developed during the four days of the seminar.

To all those who have continued the process of personal growth through leadership programs 1, 2 and 3.

To the children and teenagers who have participated in the seminars of Avante.

To those who are part of our great AVANTE family.

To God, for using us as a tool to teach the power of forgiveness.

With our love and gratitude,

Clara y Mirna

Avante Seminars

INDEX OF TANGLES AND CHANGES

PROLOGUE

Obviously, one of the main needs for human beings is education. I am not referring solely to academics, but I do refer to learning to live, education for everyday life. We need to learn what urges us, as a society and as individuals, to know and to recognize ourselves in order to modify behaviors which constrain us, and produce suffering to those around us and ourselves. Economic and social pressures have absorbed us in such a way that we have forgotten to live. Instead, we confine ourselves to surviving. We work without enjoying, we eat without tasting, we speak without communicating, and we ride through life accepting and generating destructive, painful relationships. The worst thing about this is that we have become accustomed to living like this, and we believe that we should continue that way. The good news, which brings us this work, is that nothing compels us to live that way; and we have the right and the ability to change our destiny.

Life, as Mirna Pineda and Clara Arenas say, is simple and also full of opportunities. Today I had the wonderful opportunity to read and enjoy the excellent work of these excavators of the conscience and human behavior. Additionally, they have allowed me the honor of sharing my views about this book. In recommendation of this reading, I would like to thank the authors for the great contribution that, once more, is a favor to all of us. The transforming content of their seminars "The Challenge of Changing Your Life" is now within the reach of everyone through this book which, like the workshops, they share with simple and understandable language. No longer will it be necessary move to Phoenix, Arizona to receive their concepts, ideas and proposals for a change of thought and, with it, of life.

Blessed is the day that these two women met. Although their origins were separated by thousands of kilometers, they were created with a fully compatible emotional, professional and spiritual DNA, of sisters, not of blood, but of life. It is the kind of sisterhood, which does not require bonds for a surname, but of purpose. There are few times we can find in the intellectual world colleagues who can combine so well their work, not only as teammates, but as true friends. Such is the case of Clara and Mirna. The occasions when I have worked with them, I have confirmed that their relationship is not a simple working agreement, but a mission of life in which both complement and help each other; they provide support to each other, and they have fun. Their friendship, creative collaboration and complicity constantly produce the good fruits that now are reflected in this text. In this book we can identify the transformers' hearts of these two catalysts of the human potential. Their alliance is a clear example of what they suggest in one of its chapters: to join people with skills, which complement and help us to succeed and be happy.

It gives me great pleasure to discover that they have shaped in this work much of the experience gained by their many years of work and intervention in the development of people, especially Hispanics, who live in the United States. There was an urgent need to extend and make accessible to more people the contents of their seminars and programs of change for a better quality of life. Their proposal for the transformation is not based only on the theory, but in the application of the same in hundreds of cases. Therefore we can trust that they are not speaking from a classroom and a blackboard, but from the privacy and intimacy of a kitchen, a bedroom, office, restaurant, conference room or the patio of the houses of those who have realized the benefits of approaching these women to change their destiny.

"The Challenge of Changing Your Life" is not only a stop on the way to reflecting life, happiness, our relationships, past, present, future and mainly, about ourselves, it is rather a repair and maintenance workshop which we can use to align and fix ourselves and then return to the path with another perspective, a new vision and tools to correct any damage that may arise during the rest of our journey.

I could not agree more with the opening phrase, which they used to begin their work: "life is simple; human beings tangle it up". We are specialists in complicating our existence. It would appear that many of us have believed that the suffering, the misery, the dissatisfaction and the limitations are an inevitable part of our destiny. We have forgotten that life is not a painful path to walk, but one of learning, joy and growth, in spite of the challenges which arise.

Our tangles are not greater than our ability to untangle them; however, we need help to achieve this. We require that people like Mirna and Clara remind us of that and give us the tools to prove it. There is no way out of this tangled existence by repeating the same approaches forever; but to change, we must first change our way of thinking, our beliefs, and our infamous and, many times, wrong paradigms. It is of little use to us to modify our behaviors if we continue to believe that we are incapable of having a better way of life, that have to endure, that our happiness depends on others or that it is God's plan to keep us within our current way of life.

The pages of this book are like mirrors and windows of the soul. The first allow us to identify all these invisible auto limitations that we carry on our backs with all their consequences. Each tangle explains to us how we find the mental, emotional and relational knots within which we have enclosed ourselves, or which we have inherited. The approaches of these two women show us uncomfortable and disadvantageous realities to which we have become accustomed, forgetting that we have the possibility to leave them to find a better way to spend every day of our existence. In the stories that they share about the people whom they have helped to transform and grow, we find similarities to our own lives, experiences and tangles. Our "acute victimitis" is exposed and visible within the explanations that they give us and the examples and testimonies which they describe. The good thing is that, along with the mirrors, they open windows to show us that there is hope; that we are not destined to live forever with these sufferings and attitudes. Through these crystals we can see the mental models that they propose to us to unleash our existential knots and modify our destiny. As well, with each tangle that they expose they also offer a thought about a transformation, which gives us the solution to break down those ideas that have limited our life and, with this, the happiness to live it.

In your hands, dear reader, you have a compendium of information which can change your life. These sheets offer practical, realistic, and effective alternatives to put an end to attitudes and thoughts that have imprisoned our happiness. Our past does not have to continue to determine our present and future, if we can transform our lives. We have an excellent text to discover and rediscover the new horizons which give us the freedom of personal responsibility.

I invite you to take advantage of this opportunity that life gives us through Clara and Mirna to make a positive rethinking of our way of living. Its realistic optimism encourages you to see things from a perspective of growth, learning, and happiness in spite of the circumstances. Read it with the certainty that there is hope to reach a different, better and more satisfactory destination. Let's have the audacity to look at ourselves through these mirrors of the conduct without fear, and look through its windows toward the options for change that will lead us to an extraordinary existence. The positive transformation of our lives, and of our relations, is within the scope of our mind and a few sheets of distance.

Rafael Ayala

Motivator of consciousness

ACKNOWLEDGEMENTS

CONNECTING THE DOTS

I was very small when I received some drawing books, which by connecting the dots, revealed a wonderful design.

The same had happened in my life.

I studied the career of Communication looking for better ways of interacting with others. I love my profession because it has given me the opportunity to put into practice the idea that "the media is not good or bad, all depends on how you use it".

Simultaneously, with the journalistic practice I started to give classes, with the purpose of easing the path of the new generations of journalists and professionals in general. When I completed the Master's Degree in Education with a specialty in communication, I had not even imagined the wonderful potential that would open up, years later, to implement the learning. Combining both careers has been a cornerstone of my personal development and, of course, professional.

I was starting to connect the dots.

I have known Clara for centuries, long before reaching this world. There are so many coincidences - as Rafael Ayala well annotated: "they are sisters of life"- We started to be partners when we found empathy in a passion for teaching. The ways have been different, the purpose is the same: to plant seeds of improvement to elevate the consciousness.

There is no perfect formula in personal relations or business. What is certain is that to make them functional it is necessary to open the mind and the heart to learn from one another, with the belief of "emptying the glass" so that it can be filled with new ideas to enrich that were already inside.

Clara honors her name, is "transparent, bright, clean and pure feelings". She is my mentor, teacher, friend, partner, with whom I laughed, cried and learned.

I am sure that there is a spiritual covenant between us. It took several more years before discovering that Clara was born the same day as Paulita, my mother. In addition, Alberto – Clara's husband - has the same birthday date as Alfonso, my dad.

My husband says that I have adoptive parents; I say that those are part of the covenants I was not aware of that give me the opportunity to continue learning.

Thanks Clara for coexisting in my life.

Humberto, - my husband and partner - represents many of the points of connection in my life. Thanks to his patience and support I have been able to create a more harmonious present. He put up with stoicism my bad moods when I had not unraveled the tangles of my past -and still have not finished. I am still on the road, because forgiveness is a process and I keep making mistakes - Don't be scared Humberto. Every time I throw fewer temper tantrums.

As I wrote in the previous book, IDEAS TO MOVE FORWARD, Humberto is not my half orange, he is the complete orange. He is not my prince charming, and I am not his princess, but he is my ideal partner.

Thank you Humberto for being, doing and having.

Paulina and Marianne are the result of that communion. They are the mirror where I am reflected, the engine that drives me to continue learning. I didn't get the manual to be a "good mom" and I believe that if I had received it I would have not read it since I don't like to follow instructions.

Thank you my stars, because you are God's gifts.

About 17 years ago, I met Rafael Ayala. At the time he was a young boy - my age - who devoted part of his time to do community service at his church by giving talks to adolescents. In addition to running a news broadcast on television every night, -and in my eagerness to share with the public what I was beginning to learn in the area of human development- I took to the task of producing and running another program, also television, which was baptized with the name of EXCELLENT, through TELEMAX a TV channel of Sonora Mexico which became my house and my school for thirteen years. The program involved specialists and cognoscenti of personal development. I invited Rafael, and during the pre-production I asked him which main problems the young people they worked with faced. He told me that their home situations: violence, addiction, lack of communication. All of this left deep wounds in their souls.

The theme of the program arose from that answer: WOUNDS OF THE SOUL and sometime later it became the title of the first book by Rafael. For many years we have had sporadic electronic communications, until we got back to "connect the dots" and join wills in our mutual passion for teaching the raising of consciousness.

Rafael Ayala is a wonderful motivator of consciousness; a human being that explores and shares, and knows that healing the wounds opened the doors to a transformational present.

The invitation to write the foreword to the book came as a bold idea that I shared with Clara and we clicked in the same instant. Rafael received it with humility and gratitude and responded with a great gift.

Thanks Rafa for sharing.

To my esteemed Marent, a man of unlimited creativity and open smile, I owe a hilarious interview that put me in the newspaper first page in 1999. I respected him more when we worked together with my beloved director DON FORTINO LEON ALMADA on the newspaper "El

Sonorense" To Don Fortino I give my affection, respect, gratitude and permanent love, despite his untimely and precipitous death.. He continues to be my adoptive dad simply because he decided to "adopt" me as his daughter.

Marent is a fun, sarcastic and fine guy. I have admired him ever since I read his comic strip PERRO PERO (DOG, BUT). Marent and Perro Pero have perfect smiles, Could it be coincidence?

We sailed through the murky waters of journalism, but Marent is also a designer - of dreams and illusions - When we re-connected and I raised the idea of illustrating the book, he was quick to grab control of the project and began the doing and undoing electronically, I keep laughing when I re-read them. Mario Renteria -Marent-, has extraordinary talents. I told him I don't know if I enjoy most his cartoons or his writings. He replied to keep what gives me peace. Then I decided to stay with the two. It is a gift to the senses.

Thank you, Maren for always smiling.

When I published my first book, "7 Soles", in 2007, a novel about the trafficking of persons and undocumented immigration, based on a film script, a person sent me a message telling me that she liked the beautiful work very much. She offered some grammatical corrections to improve the second edition. Marina Ruiz made the corrections for the pleasure of doing it. Then we hired her to make the grammatical corrections of the book IDEAS PARA SEGUIR AVANTE (Ideas to Move Forward), and finally I met her in person, five years after our first e-mail. She is a lovely and charming woman, neat in both speaking and writing, concerned that the ideas carry the appropriate accents. She lives as a grandmother who reviews texts "to make money for her chewing gum" she says with an open smile.

Thank you, Marina, for living.

Core Parts, my mother Paulita and my dad Alfonso, source of origin and development. Thank you for everything that you gave me. Today

I realize that was what they had and knew. I honor their inheritance. Focal points my brothers Rosy, Alfonso and Diana, I love them as well and I treat them differently, because they are different, always near despite the distance. Thanks for blooming and bearing fruit in Alex, Tone, Paola, Poncho, Diana, Sara and Daniela. My gratitude to Perla and Pedro for being there. Beloved friends, Blanca, Jossie, Irene, Lupita, Sylvia, companions of school and work, friends for life, uncles, cousins, family in law, teachers, students. How much to thank in this time shared!

And the dots keep connecting. There is a long list of people who have been part of AVANTE SEMINARS, who have belief and trust. It would be too risky to write each name, for the fear of leaving anyone out. All of them are wonderful beings, a large group with whom we have brotherhood relationships that make our family bigger. That they are immigrants is a great gift, because we are never physically alone. They also love the fiesta and look for any excuse to continue celebrating life.

Thanks to each and every one of you for giving me the opportunity to share the learning and the teachings. When I teach, I learn twice..

The connectivity between all, extraordinary human beings circumstances, cities, opportunities, experiences, have resulted in the book that you now have in front of you. The tangles and ideas expressed here are not dogmas of faith nor absolute truths. You don't have to agree or disagree with anything that is expressed here. Take or discard what you think might be useful for your life, with the purpose of being at peace with yourself.

For my part, I will share my ideas and learning with those who wish to cultivate change.

I am the result of the seeds that others have planted in me, coupled with my own deductions and interpretations.

I will continue drawing new ideas in my mind, untangling the tangles of my soul, forgiving and being happy. Thanks for the opportunity to continue connecting the points.

Blessings in abundance to your life.

God is always first.

Mirna Pineda-Acuña

An extraordinary day in the month of April 2012

GRATITUDE TO MY TEACHERS

When Mirna asked me to write the acknowledgments I went back to my native country: Colombia, my roots and history and a story filled with teachers who came to my life in different shapes, sizes and occasions, who offered me learning opportunities in the form of experiences, some pleasant, others not so much. And sometimes, perhaps it was I who came to their lives, consciously or unconsciously, because when the pupil is ready, the teacher appears. All of these teachings are the ones that allow me to write this book today and share part of my journey with the readers.

My deepest and most sincere thanks to all my teachers. I would love to mention them all, however, due to space considerations, I will mention them in groups.

My first teachers are certainly my parents, with whom I learned the value of work, honesty, perseverance, faith, and to find the good in everything. Thanks to their imperfections I learned tolerance, understanding and compassion. They were not perfect parents, but they were the perfect parents for me to get the necessary learning that would prepare me to fulfill my life mission. Today I can say that I love and accept them as they are.

Growing up with four sisters and three brothers was not an easy task, especially for them. Even when on many occasions I was the good girl for convenience, I was mischievous once in a while in my search for acceptance and recognition. We quarreled at times and in others we protected each other.. I learned from them the value of friendship, of teamwork, of helping and looking after each other, in spite of the distance. We were complicit many times. Today the love that unites us helps keep me learning and teaching, because I know that they rely on me and see me as a model for their lives.

My family keeps up to date and therefore continues to grow in number and knowledge. The commitment with them helps me to keep moving forward, and that commitment was a great motivation for writing this book. Even when we are physically far away, they are always in my heart.

Some teachers come into our lives for a short time and others stay for a long time. My life partner since I was 16 years old, has been a wonderful tool for my personal growth; he shared with me my intolerance, my rage, my pain, my fear, my insecurity. Fortunately he had enough patience to see and also to share my love, tolerance, security, trust, compassion and above all the peace that I was acquiring as my wounds were healing. With my husband, Alberto, I dreamed, traveled and learned the value of perseverance, discipline, the method. When he shared with me his dreams of traveling to the United States to learn, to know different places and to seek a better life, I could not imagine that by deciding to follow and support him in this attempt I would find the way for my healing and the direction my life would take.

The main source of inspiration for all of my work has been my beautiful children: Cynthia Gigliola, Noelia Celeste and Renzo Omar. They arrived at different times of my spiritual development, each one bringing with him/her a message for me.

This book is one more tool to fulfill the dream of leaving for them a world of peace, and of creating a legacy for them and future generations. Thank you, my dears, for having chosen me as your mom. Thank you for having taught me what unconditional love and forgiveness is. Thank you for believing and trusting in me.

Many other teachers have come to my life through books or audio-visual material, in seminars, workshops, conferences; sometimes in casual conversations and other times as my personal mentors. They taught me many of the ideas that today I share in these pages, they encouraged me to put them into practice, and so they showed me the way out of the darkness to light, from depression to happiness, from hatred to love. I have learned to be happy despite … and I feel that the best way to thank them is to continue passing the message.

My most sincere gratitude also goes to Marina for her patience in checking and correcting these pages in Spanish, Marent by sharing his good sense of humor and his cartoonish ability, which facilitates the transmission of the message, and Rafael Ayala for taking the time, in spite of all his occupations, to write the foreword. The three I met through my dear friend Mirna who has shared with me the mutual respect and affection that exists between them.

When Mirna and I decided to translate the book into English and I volunteered to take the task on my own hands, I knew I was going to need a kind, caring and very professional person to review and correct my job. Her name came to my mind immediately. I shared my decision with my oldest daughter and she said: "She is the best in the world, her English is wonderful, she is very professional and her kindness, trust and caring attitude is one of a kind". I met Paula Banda about 12 years ago, just a few months after arriving in Arizona to start a new episode in my life. Thanks, Paula, for accepting this challenge with your usual optimism and loving heart.

My gratitude for all the people who have arrived at Avante, either for a short time or who have stayed to share with us your personal growth and to help us to deliver the message. You are and make a difference, starting at your hearts and extending it to your families, neighbors, cities and the entire world. Wonderful people came to Avante Seminars in search of something better, looking for peace and freedom. Thanks to who believed in God, in themselves and in us, and who shared a slice of their life leaving huge teachings in ours. Divine beings having human experiences that on their way back to the Creator, coincide in the lives of Mirna and me allowing us to share our knowledge, our experiences and facilitating us to be teachers and students at the same time.

This book could not become a reality without the love, dedication, perseverance, faith, and gentile harassment of my partner and friend Mirna Pineda. These words of appreciation are also accompanied by my love and my respect for a person of integrity and humbleness, who believed and whose dream to bring the message of change and peace to the world harmonize with mine. This allowed us to create Avante Seminars. What started as a partnership was quickly transformed into a friendship. Mirna has become my spiritual partner, my friend. Thanks for believing and creating, for loving and forgiving, for living in excellence, for dreaming and sharing your dreams, for teaching and learning, for being student and teacher, for your faith and simplicity. Simply thank you for being.

Thanks to a wonderful and wise human being, Paula Leonard, who patiently reviewed the translation of the book.

Thanks, God, for using me as an instrument to deliver the message of peace and forgiveness.

Clara Arenas

INTRODUCTION

Life is simple; we humans tangle it up.

We make knots where there are straight lines, we spend our time suffering for things that can't be fixed, and we do not sleep because we attempt to solve our economic problems. If we could pay our debts by not sleeping, the streets would be full of zombies.

We make complicated tangles pulling our ideas from side to side, fighting with what we were told was right or wrong, without even questioning if those ideas work for us or not.

We get attached to old habits because it is all we know; however, that does not mean those habits are the only ones that exist. There are many ways to do things and sometimes we don't even realize there are other ways. People get so attached to their habits that they believe that is the only right way. That is the reason it is important to change.

Change occurs, whether you like it or not.

Every second there is change internally and externally. Your cells change at every instant, some regenerate, some multiply and some die. Pessimists say that every day is the same; however, the reality is that there aren't two exact days that are the same.

In many cases the changes are so subtle that they're hard to notice. Suddenly we go on the bathroom scale and "zap" there are five more pounds that were not there a few months ago. We pull on a pair of pants from the closet, and we think they have shrunk because the buttons do not close anymore. We look in the mirror and there we can see the wrinkles that started to make their way years ago. We go back to our native city and find more boulevards and many new faces, too. We don't even recognize our neighbors!

You just start to learn how to read and there are neuronal changes. There are processes in your mind so you can continue reading.

So if we change each minute, why do we have so much resistance to changing our life?

During our years of working with people on self-development, it surprises us to hear people say that they are "not ready" to change, despite the fact that we change every single minute.

Fear is the real reason why people refuse to work on themselves.

They are afraid of what there is inside.

They prefer to live mediocre lives, have mediocre relationships, and allow their children to imitate their mediocrity, because that is the only thing the children know. When people get invited to participate in experiential seminars, where they can work on the origin of their limitations, make substantial changes and make decisions that can help them to find inner peace, they argue and insist that it is not their time.

If we wait for the right moment to change, we will be losing the most valuable thing we have: that NOW.

When are we ever 100% prepared?

The reality is that we are never fully prepared for a new task. If we wait until we are totally prepared to be parents, the birth rate of the world would lower dramatically. If we wait to be completely prepared to drive a car, there would be fewer automobiles on the roads and maybe fewer accidents.

We gain experience through practice, and with practice come mistakes, bloopers, which in reality are only great opportunities to test our talents and give us the chance to learn from them and live in excellence.

To be excellent does not mean to be perfect, but it means to be willing to make mistakes. To be excellent is to accept the errors, correct them, and avoid making the same ones over and over again.

The purpose is to elevate our consciousness so we can see what is going on inside us, instead of blaming other for our feelings.

Of course, it is easier and more comfortable to blame others. However the only one responsible for our happiness or unhappiness is ourselves.

Nobody else is.

To accept an error, to be open and humbly say "I made a mistake", to recognize that we have a problem is one of the first steps to becoming conscious of our actions and results. Because to elevate our consciousness it is important to remember that there is a sacred right, and it is the right to make mistakes. A bigger one is to forgive.

To forgive ourselves is the first step to reaching our happiness.

In this book we share with you the topics and experiences that we have accumulated during our time facilitating a four day seminar THE CHALLENGE OF CHANGING YOUR LIFE, an intense experiential program that give tools to initiate the inner changes. The program is the results of the union of information obtained by the authors during their 20 years of experience in leadership, team group, image development, oral and corporal communication education, as well as physical therapy practice.

The working plan adds up the knowledge of people who have influenced our lives, because we are the result of each one of the multiple seeds that were planted in our minds.

We also include some of the topics that we developed in the other programs such as Leadership levels 1, 2 and 3. The first two are 3-month programs and the last one is a 2-month program. During the leadership programs, the participants' concrete actions started to evolve during the first seminar through AVANTE SEMINARS, Training for Your Life.

The purpose of our company is to help people to reach success through the development of their potential.

Our main objective is to share tools that make it possible to spread the message of FORGIVENESS.

FORGIVENESS is the core of our work and the main key to achieving inner peace.

Our goal is to give you the tools that will allow you to enjoy your inner potential. If you want to untangle the knots that you build in your mind, all you have to do is to decide and accept THE CHALLENGE TO CHANGE YOUR LIFE.

TANGLE: I WILL BE HAPPY WHEN
CHANGE: I AM HAPPY EVEN THOUGH

TANGLE:
I WILL BE HAPPY WHEN

CHANGE:
I'M HAPPY EVEN THOUGH

If you had a magic wand and you could ask for 3 wishes, what would you wish for?

You have 10 seconds to say them aloud.

10, 9, 8, 7, 6, 5, 4, 3, 2, 1 ¡Time!

Even though the phrase sounds like a story, it is interesting to note that when we ask this question to the participants of our seminar, hardly ever can somebody define more than one wish. Some of them openly affirm that they do not know what they want. Some others murmur something like: "I want to be happy". And they say it very quietly.

They have spent their lives looking for happiness, and on the road they have found only sorrows. They look outside themselves: waiting to be grownups in order to be happy, when school is over, when they get married (for some when they get divorced), when their partner changes and makes them happy. They wait to win the lottery, so they can be debt free. They wait for their children to grow up, so they have time to travel. Then and only then they will have all they have been waiting for; then they think they will be happy.

People connect their happiness to WHEN.

What about a new idea: what about starting by making the changes in your mind?

Instead of waiting to be happy WHEN, be happy EVEN THOUGH.

Because being happy is an inner decision, it does not depend on circumstances.

To be able to declare: "Even though I do not have the car of my dreams, I decide to be happy". "Even though I have a headache, I decide to be happy". "Even though a loved one just died, I have decided to be happy".

If we say that, the workshop participants' eyes open wide, and we almost can read their faces: "If it were so easy." "They do not know my story". "MY LIFE HAS BEEN SO DIFFICULT". "It is easy for them to say that, but if they knew my story …!"

It is true that the life stories are diverse; the events can change. However, the emotions are the same: guilt, shame, sadness, depression, pessimism, envy, jealousy, boredom, anger, resentment. An accumulation of negative emotions tends to be limiting, and in general they distort the perception and interpretation of the facts. It also discourages people from reaching their goals, prompting them to inactivity, passivity, and in many cases to aggressiveness.

The important thing is that when people can define at least one wish —which can be obtained with the mental magic wand-, and decide to work on themselves, a great number of people mention an emotion, this time positive such as happiness, satisfaction, hope, plenitude, good humor, optimism, tranquility and peace as part of what they want to get for their lives.

"I want to be happy", they say with a quiet voice. They look at what others say, because they feel that they have failed and that they are the only ones that feel that way. When they realize that they are not alone, that everybody else in the group feels the same, they give a sigh of relief. Then some of them say smiling: "Well, it seems like we all want the same, but we do not know how to get it."

What they don't realize is that they have already started to find the way. You are doing the same by reading this book. You are beginning to move forward instead of remaining stuck.

The next expression is heard frequently during the seminars, the only difference is the person's name or sex. It can come out of a mouth of a woman or a man: "Life is soooo difficult." They lengthen the word "so" to make it more emphatic.

"Who said it was difficult?" We ask.

Then they start to tell all the stories that they heard, the phrases that somebody else mentioned over and over again, part of the legacy from their parents, family members, friends, teachers, etc. The most interesting thing is that they take it as truth, because "everybody" said so.

Instead of labeling life according to "How you have done so far?" according to your own experiences, and the ones that were given to you for generations, add this new idea to your mind:

LIFE IS ...

Everyone needs to finish the sentence. Life can be as beautiful as you want to see it, or as tragic as you decide, depending on individual perception and interpretation. The marvelous Celia Cruz used to sing with all her heart that "Anyone who thinks life is cruel, needs to know that it is not true, there are only bad moments, and everything passes. Life is a carnival to laugh and enjoy".

Life is a game with no instructions; and if it had them, most likely we wouldn't read or practice them anyway.

This brings up another phrase made popular by a communicator: "The media is not good or bad; it depends on the use that it will be given". We could paraphrase Marshall McLuhan and affirm that LIFE IS NOT GOOD OR BAD, IT DEPENDS ON HOW WE USE IT.

If we talk about the use, the simplest way is to look at results. If you are happy with them, if the results make you feel complete, happy and in peace, GO AHEAD! Keep working on yourself because the road is long and lasts for the rest of your life. If you think you know it all, then it is time to buy your coffin because that means you are ready to die. You could be one of those who conform to the results and feel "comfortable"; you do what you think you can, not what you REALLY CAN do, because you are afraid of growing.

If on the contrary, your results provoke a state of altercation, irritability, nervousness, agitation, constant fear, shame, hostility and affliction, it is time to make changes in your life.

As a consolation, most of people who live around you share the same negative emotions. Only 1% of the world population lives in a state of integral consciousness. The rest of the population is on a constant quest for illusions, power, order, autonomy, liberty, abundance and peace. There is a need and there are resources and tools that can be used to start this work.

People look for changes in order to do different things, because what they have now does not produce actual satisfactory results. And yes, there are ways to change. The evidence is in the people who have participated in the personal development seminars.

Also we are proof that we have made substantial changes in our lives after participating in multiple seminars, workshops, conferences, mentorships, and advisers. We also have received instruction in order to be able to teach. Our way to see the world is different, and now we know that it is possible to have inner peace in spite of the stories of the past.

To face ourselves frightens us. We have been trained, since early childhood, to point outside of ourselves. It is easy to believe that everybody else needs to change.

A young couple that had frequent complicated situations attended one of our seminars. Ana insisted that her family was to blame for her depression, because every time she wanted to do something new, all she heard was: "Why are you wasting your time, you don't even have any education", "You have always been so dumb", "You only know how to cook, so just go back to the kitchen", "Women who wander on their own become prostitutes". She got very upset when we told her that she was responsible for her feelings, because she has the ability to accept or reject the family comments.

Everybody else promptly realized that what we were saying was true. They agreed, except her. However, later, other participants who had agreed insisted that their cases were different.

Jorge explained that his situation was different, because his partner did not allow him to be happy; she criticized him constantly, even in front of the children. She used to tell him: "You are useless, and never do anything right. I have to solve everything because you are unable to do anything." According to Jorge, his partner was responsible for how he felt. She was a victimizer, and he was the victim.

There is a disease that is becoming epidemic. Its name is ACUTE VITIMITIS. It is very contagious and hereditary. This disease can be passing from generation to generation. If you don't believe this, just pay attention to the next phrases: "Look at this grey hair; it is because all the problems you give me!" "You have no consideration for me even after all the SACRIFICES I made for you!" "I kill myself working so hard so I can give you everything, and this is the way you repay me?"

Do they sound familiar? Are these the phrases you have heard or the ones you say? If you heard them, and you have not made inner changes in your life, then most probably you are repeating them.

How many times have you said to yourself: "I WILL NEVER become like my parents and WILL NEVER do the same as they did to me"?

We invite you to look at your results, so that you can honestly say that you are not doing the same. Pay attention, the form can be different but the results can be the same.

Marina came into one of the workshops crossing her arms and legs. She participated with determination, with a strong voice and a fixed look, and we could say with some anger. At one point, she shared with the group that when she was a child she was physically abused by her stepfather. She used to go to her grandmother bleeding and almost fainting. Her grandmother usually cured her wounds. The physical punishment was non-stop, so she decided to run away from home when she was thirteen years old. She swore that from that day on, she was not going to allow a man to hurt her, and that nobody would tell her what to do, that she was going to do whatever pleased her. Some years later she met the guy who became her husband. He was a nice, kind, gentleman and he was madly in love with her. When the problems began and they had discussions, she was the one who verbally and physically abused him.

Marina had made changes. Now it was not the man who originated the violence, she was the aggressor; she was imitating the behavior that caused her so much suffering.

Her children learned the relationship model, and they had abusive relationships too, some of them being the aggressor and others becoming the victims. That was all they knew.

The form changed, but the result was the same.

The sexual, physical, emotional and financial abuse becomes a chain; it is given as part of our heritage for ourselves, unless we make real inner changes at the subconscious level.

If you are not pleased with your present results, then it is time to do something different. The definition of insanity is to do the same over and over expecting different results.

Ask yourself: Am I crazy?

How long have you been dissatisfied with your results and still keep doing the same thing over and over?

How long are you still going to wait before giving yourself the opportunity to be happy?

We were surprised by the comment of one of the participants who lived in a domestic violence situation: "I can't do it anymore." "I want to get divorced." "I am fed up with this." "I have tolerated this for so many years that I do not want the same!" Then she paused for a couple of seconds and lowered her voice to continue: "But I have spent ten years of my life with him, how am I going to throw that away so easily?" We questioned her: "So, do you want to live another ten years like that?"

In extreme situations, it is recommendable that couples break up, not to miss each other or to decide if they need each other, but to work on themselves, improve their lives, heal the past and build a different present.

It is proven that when couples divorce or separate without making inner changes, they usually find another identical partner just with a different name. This is so because wherever they go, even if they change homes, county or partners, they take themselves with them.

If you are reading this book it means you are looking for something different. We suggest that not only read the book but practice what you learn.

You have to apply this information so it becomes knowledge.

TANGLE: I WILL BELIEVE IT WHEN I SEE IT
CHANGE: I WILL SEE IT WHEN I BELIEVE IT

TANGLE:

SEEING IS BELIEVING

CHANGE:

BELIEVING IS SEEING

We are what we think.

When we think that things are difficult, everything works out to be that way so we reinforce that idea which most likely is not ours, but it was planted in our mind long time ago.

However we believe it is true and we create outcomes based on that idea.

Everything we think about can become reality. The reality exists when you are creating it. That is your reality.

The mind is a beautiful instrument that is not located only in the brain. Each one of our cells has memory. The ideas originate in the mind and provoke emotions, which in turn yield actions and the actions generate results. When you are not satisfied with the results, it is necessary to make changes in your mind so you get different results.

If you create changes, you are on the path of inner peace and when you are at peace with yourself then you are at peace with others.

We can make reality everything we think about, and it is as easy as just changing our thoughts. We can think positively or negatively. If we concentrate on the fact that we have not seen our family in a long time, we get sad and cry. Or, we remember an incident when someone said something we interpreted as aggressive, and our mind starts going around with the same idea: "Why did he/she say that?", "She is up to something, I did not do anything to him/her; she/he must be in trouble". We keep going on and on until we make ourselves sick and/or throw a tantrum. Our actions change due to that idea that got us in a bad mood, and we lash out at those who have nothing to do with the problem, usually our kids.

The kids are in their own world, and mom may be thinking about what she is going to tell her husband for being late. Her mind is filled with ideas like: "The bum (or let's use "good for nothing") is late, I'll wait and see what excuse he comes up with this time! This time he is going to hear me, don't even think I am going to believe his story". At that moment the little kid asks "Mom, can I eat a piece of cake? Mom's reaction is: "NO! Stop bothering me! How many times do I have to say no? Get out of here, you are in time out!" The child asks himself, "What did I do? I just wanted some cake!"

Our actions determine our results, and the results do work or not –let's start changing the idea about results being good or bad, positive or negative, when we do a detailed review of the outcomes of our actions in the four basic areas: emotional, physical, financial and spiritual let's focus on how functional they are.

Remember that everything that became reality was first just an idea in someone's mind. This book that you are reading came about first in the author's mind. The chair where you are sitting right now was first just someone's idea. Somebody designed the house where you live, and then somebody else built it. You decorated it, but first you thought of where the furniture and the pictures were going to be. You thought of every single detail, even when you said "I do not like the way it looks.

I have not had time to organize". When you put it there, for whatever reason, you imagined it first.

Somebody imagined the marvelous New York skyscrapers and the impressive architectural and engineering masterpieces of the world. Where did the construction begin? In the mind, and then it became reality. All the inventions we have now which facilitate our lives, like computers and cell phones, did not exit a few decades ago. Today we can't image our lives without a computer or a cell phone. At the beginning computers were huge; they occupied a whole floor in a building and cell phones looked like bricks. Someone had the idea that these artifacts could be small, portable and comfortable. They imaged them, then they made them a physical reality and those inventors became famous millionaires!

Everything we think, absolutely everything, good or bad, can be made a physical reality. If we focus only on the bad, then we know where we are going to end up.

The only one responsible for the results is you, even though you usually give the control –like a TV remote control- to everyone and everything around you.

If you wait for the world to change, it is going to take a long time; start the changes within you; it is only a matter of a decision.

Some people resist the change, they say: "That's the way I am; and if people don't like it, that's their problem." They spend most of the time throwing tantrums, insulting, cursing, hitting with words and actions, getting sick and making everybody around them sick.

It is hard to live with that type of person, and it is worse to BE that way.

This was the discovery that one of the seminar participants made at the end of the program. She exclaimed: "I am sorry for my husband. It is ugly to live with someone like me. I had not even noticed what I was doing and saying; I thought I was always right and that he was doing things to bother me. Now I understand he does things in a different way, because he is different than me".

Just as you are expecting others to change, they are hoping you are the one who will change.

You receive what you give, it is a Universal law. We want to give you the secret recipe so you don't waste your time: Start with you.

It is that simple. When you change, everything changes, because you start to see, feel, enjoy, perceive and interpret things differently. When you change your thoughts, you change your ideas. Immediately, your emotions change and so do your actions; therefore your results will vary, too.

One of the participants on our radio show commented "If I do not take the pills, I get depressed". She had created that need at a mental level; if she did not take the pill she got depressed. She conditioned her emotions.

Another participant had a similar story. She used to take 5 to 6 pills each day because of her depression, anxiety and beginning schizophrenia. While doing one of the exercises, she realized she was going over and over the same story. She believed she was a victim of circumstances while she was growing up. As an adult, she kept repeating the same pattern expecting her family to see her as the victim. She was using this behavior to bribe them and to get what she wanted. . When things did not go her way, she got sick and blamed her family: "She worked so hard for everybody, and they did not pay attention to her". This pattern became an illness cycle: prescription drugs, messed up emotions. Finally, she became a legal drug addict until she realized the only one responsible for her results was herself. When she finished her inner work at the seminar, she quit her medicines, and she has not needed them anymore.

What if you start now to change your thoughts? How can you do it? The first thing you need to do is to look inside yourself. In the previous case, it was necessary to find the root of the depression, what were the thoughts that depressed her. The drugs relieved the symptom, but it did not take care of the cause.

You need to be aware that everything you think about with emotion, you can make a reality; it is important to ask yourself: what do I want to make reality, the positive or the negative? To believe is to create.

Rosalba believed she was shy. She heard that many times at home while growing up. Then, she was told again at school by her teachers. Later on she married a man who reconfirmed her belief. She behaved like a shy person for years. Her life results did not satisfy her, and she was not happy. When she finally decided to change, she started to go to seminars, read books and get together with different people. To her surprise, she realized how extroverted she was, and little by little she began to behave confidently. Today she has friends, expresses her feelings easily, and her life is changing. Her transformation began with the change in her beliefs.

And you? What do you want to create in your life? What do you want to believe?

TANGLE: I MARRY THE OLD IDEAS
CHANGE: I AM OPEN TO CHANGE

TANGLE:

I MARRY THE OLD IDEAS

CHANGE:

I AM OPEN TO CHANGE

There is a belief that old is better. People say that there was respect, civility, fewer robberies, less crime in the old days. The truth is that not all old times were better and while civilization keeps changing, values remain the same. The way we apply those values is different or we just don't apply them at all.

However many people literally marry their values with those old ideas because it gives them the excuse necessary to stay still. For example: "It is imperative to punish children so they will learn".

Physical punishment creates fear and resentment. Parents hit their kids, pull their hair, pinch them, slap them on the face, because that was what they received while growing up. That is the only way the parents know. It is important to clarify that there is a difference between discipline and punishment. Beatings are physical and emotional abuse. Maybe the little kid won't make the same mischief or mistake, not because he/she understands and manages the experience, but because of the terror of the punishment and the fear of more beatings. They grow up with fear. However, when they become parents they have the tendency to hit too, thus continuing with the chain of abuse.

It is important to learn new ideas, so we can decide which ones we want, why these ideas work, which ones do not work, and why they limit our freedom to be happy.

When a human being hears a new idea, he/she has the tendency to do one of these three things:

1. **Ignore it**

   Teenagers are really good at that and they use phrases such as: "Whatever", "who cares", and they shrug their shoulders.

2. **Accept it**

   If the new idea is in alignment with those which are programmed in their minds, or they identify themselves with the person sharing the new idea, for example a figure in a TV commercial where the famous artist or player speaks out about a product.

3. **Reject it**

   Automatically if they feel attacked as it happens often during adolescence. When teenagers are on their own quest, they do not accept restrictions from their parents or teachers.

We invite you to analyze the new ideas we are going to present to you in this book. The next three questions can serve as a guide:

- Will the application of this idea help me to reach my goals, and become a better person?

- Does this idea align with the Universal laws or God's laws —whatever your concept of God is-, not from the religious stand point, but from the spiritual angle, understanding that we are spiritual beings having a physical experience?

- If I implement this idea am I going to hurt someone? When we talk about hurting someone, we are not referring to the fact that we are going to make people uncomfortable on purpose. As you start changing, doing different things, growing, untangling the mess that occupies your mind, it is possible that those close to you will get uneasy feelings.

Ernesto came to one of our workshops and decided he was going to take the four day seminar. He called the office a week later and said he was not going to be able to attend the seminar because his family got upset with him. They warned him not to get "into those things" because that was a "coco wash". Also they told him that there was nothing wrong with his life. They insisted that he thank God for everything and to resign because they were "modest" and "those things". They were referring to personal growth as being just for "rich and documented people". According to them, the undocumented did not have that "privilege".

When you make up your mind to get out of the comfort zone, those who share it with you get scared. It feels like an earthquake. They have been living as they are for a long time and have become used to it. If, for example, they live in domestic violence, they know that when the partner is in a bad mood, he is going to yell, insult and hit. They know, too, that after a while he is going to repent and ask for forgiveness. This will give them a "false" sense of certainty and the hope that tomorrow will be different. "The certainty of a bad known situation is better than an unknown good one" or isn't it?

"The fear to change is real." Or better said: the fear that someone changes us is real. We have been conditioned to conform, to dream small or not to dream at all, to go fearfully through life to make it safely to death. To change is risky, we have no idea what waits for us at the end of the road or on the road itself. However, we do know what's in it for us if we stay stuck.

We fool ourselves pretending we know the answers. A lot of people live in mediocrity due to a false sense of security. Helen Keller —deaf-mute from when she was 19 months old- said that security is a myth and wrote in her biography: "During these dark and silent years, God has been using my life for a purpose that I do not know, but that one day I will understand and I will be satisfied". Meanwhile she dedicated her life to giving conferences, to writing and to helping others who had physical limitations.

There is nothing certain in this world, except death. The real certainty lies in the understanding of the potential that God has given us. Faith in God, in ourselves, and in others provide us with true confidence.

"With luck things will remain the same and won't get worse", commented a participant when referring to her relationship with her husband. Although they had been married for 15 years, he went out with different women and was not a good provider. She not only paid for the bills, but she paid his debts. We asked her why she was still in the relationship and her answer was: "I keep hoping he will change".

After a deep analysis, she realized that the real fear was "I am afraid to be alone". Obviously, the Universe moves constantly, and it is impossible to remain the same, you move forward or backwards.

Every time she brought up the possibility of a separation, her family members remarked that it was to no avail to get divorced because "most likely she would just find a man exactly the same". Also In her mind it was planted the idea that marriage is forever. "You got married, you screwed up" they said. She had different ideas, however those other ones were holding her back.

The fear to change is real for many people. They are aware of the fact that if there are changes around them, they will have to change, too.

For example, couples tend to sleep each one on the same side of the bed all the time. Day after day, month after month, year after year, they sleep in the same position, the same way. Imagine for a minute if one of them decided to change sides; if he/she had the desire to sleep on the other side of the bed. What would happen? What would the other one feel? What paradigms would get tangled? Practice this simple idea.

The real fear is: will I be able to handle this situation?

We are not sure of our ability to handle the loss of a job, the death of a loved one, the loss of a house or a car, or just the anxiety of being alone. The feeling of loss is too strong. We were programmed that way since we were little and the media is wonderful to reinforce those ideas. There are plenty of examples of betrayal and disillusionment (loss) in songs, and the soap operas are filled with abandonment, jealousy, uncertainty, mistrust, indifference, and of course deceit; all the emotions are directed toward: FEAR. Some people prefer to endure an uncomfortable situation, weaving thousands of strands or threads of fear due to the unknown, making a blanket to cover their anxieties".

As soon as we can understand that we are able to handle any situation that we are faced with, we are ready to jump, take risks. It is not necessary to know how we are going to do it; we just need to have the certainty and the faith that we can make it.

TANGLE: THE MIND IS IN THE BRAIN
CHANGE: THE MIND DOES NOT
HAVE A SPECIFIC PLACE

TANGLE:

THE MIND IS IN THE BRAIN

CHANGE:

THE MIND HAS NO SPECIFIC PLACE

To think is to create, everything starts with thought. When you believe, you can create. Let's talk about the thoughts. How do human beings think? What is the thinking process?

Think about the word "dog", and what comes to your mind? Give yourself a few minutes to think about a dog. It can be big or small, dark or light color, or maybe it has many colors? It can be aggressive, nice or a crybaby, a dog that you already know or that you had some time ago or the one that bit you and you did not like it. The image of a dog that you build in your mind is different than the one your husband, children or neighbors have. Each person makes his/her own image of the dog. Now think about a house. Review the elements of your house: How many bedrooms? How is the garden? Or maybe it is an apartment and it has no garden. Which color is it? How many floors? Are there plants inside or outside? Your image is not the same as others, you have you own image. Now what image do you have of your "mind"?

Usually there is nothing, your mind goes blank. Many people get confused when thinking about the mind. Some say that the mind is the brain, a pink beige rubbery mass that weighs approximately 1.5 Kg, which is the center of the human nervous system. However the mind is not the brain. The mind is in each cell of our body, it is a powerful force.

We think in images, that's why it is easy to see the image of a dog, a house or a car. It is also easy to see the vacation of your dreams. However, we have no picture of the mind, which is where the real changes are made. How can we work with our mind without having an image of it? Do you think it is important to have an image of your mind, so you can understand it and work with it?

There is an image created by Dr. Thurman Fleet (1895-1983) founder of the Conceptual Therapy Institute in San Antonio, Texas, in 1934.

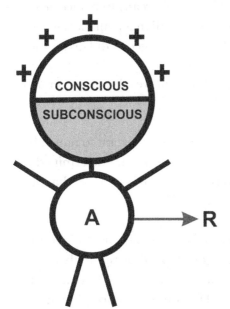

The R represents the thoughts we have in our lives. The results are in all areas emotional, spiritual, physical and financial.

The small circle represents our actions. Our actions determine our results.

The 5 crosses represent the five senses: vision, hearing, taste, smell, touch.

We are going to explain each part now.

Let's start with our results. Observe your outcomes and analyze which ones you like and which ones you do not. Your results are not the product of somebody else's actions. It is time to stop blaming others or the circumstances or external factors for the outcomes you have.

Frequently during our programs we heard the participants comment how their spouse, children, parents, government, or even the climate is responsible for their situation. Phrases like "the heat makes me angry and the cold makes me depressed", show how some people are convinced that external factors are to blame for their problems. If this is one of your beliefs you are a slave, even though you have the illusion that you are free. Someone said that it is impossible to escape from a prison if you do not know you are in one.

During a conference we gave in Mexico, a young guy who was in the first row affirmed categorically that he was not a slave because he knew exactly what he wanted and that he was doing the right things to get what he had set his mind to, which was the success of his business. When we asked him if at any point in his life someone had upset him, his immediate response was: " Of course and many times, and they still do it". We then explained to him that he was not really free since he was giving the control of his emotions to others. Until that point he had been very defensive, after that his way of thinking changed as did his attitude.

It is not easy to take responsibility for your results; however it is imperative to do it if you want to be free.

Let's continue with the image of the mind. It is important to remember that our actions determine our results. Our actions are determined by our mind, mostly by the subconscious, even though some are handled by the conscious mind.

Jose was complaining about the unbearable situation he had with his son. He was convinced that when his son stopped being stubborn and understood that his dad knew exactly what was better for him, then and only then would the situation change. The communication with his son was through screams, orders and criticism. Jose was not able to see that the outcomes with his son were simply a product of his actions.

You must be asking, "So what determines my actions?"

We function on automatic pilot most of the time. The subconscious mind controls our actions. This is good news up to certain point. It is a relief to know that, for example, when we drive we do it automatically; otherwise we would have to pay attention and know exactly at each moment when every other car crosses our way, the number of lights, etc. This would mean we would have to coordinate consciously our feet, hands, eyes, ears.

At any time in your life did you promise you were going to do something and never did? Or did you ever swear you would never do that and you did it?

Some parents understand that yelling at their kids doesn't give good results, and they promise themselves never to do it but just to talk with their children calmly. However, as soon as a situation emerges, automatically they scream like madmen. Then they reproach themselves and say things like: "I am so dumb, I know it does not work and yet I do it again".

We are going to explain later why and how this happens so you can understand how to make the changes.

Let's pay attention for a moment to the five senses.

You are used to taking information from the environment through your physical senses. You were brought up believe that the real world is limited to what you can perceive with your physical senses, that the real world is just the physical world. See it to believe it, is the common saying.

Some experts say that we perceive only 5% of the real world through the physical senses, so we are missing a lot. The reality is that we have superior faculties that allow us to access a bigger piece of the world, and that give us the opportunity to create. Remember that instead of "see it to believe it", you need to "believe it so you can see it".

Retaking Albert Einstein's idea, that imagination is more important than knowledge, we realize that using the imagination permits us to perceive a bigger world. Children have an unlimited imagination. They can travel to other countries and planets, have friends that nobody else sees, but sometimes adults say they are crazy. However, children can see it because they believe it.

While teaching at an elementary school, Clara enjoyed observing the infinite imagination of children. One time there was a drawing contest with a free theme. The children took the task very seriously and started to work. Using colors, crayons and/or pencils they expressed their imagination on paper. "When we got closer to observe seven year old Pedrito's work all we could see was a piece of paper painted in black. The other teacher asked the kid to please draw something". His answer was: "This is my drawing, don't you see it?"

Clara told the little kid: "Tell me about your drawing". His eyes lit up and he started to talk with enthusiasm about the forest with colorful trees and animals, and an enchanted house. Both Clara and Pedrito transported themselves to the world created by the boy, that others believed was only a black stain. Pedrito explained that the reason some could not see the forest was due to the fact that a magician put a spell on it and it was necessary to have "magic eyes" to see it.

Unfortunately, many adults are unable to see the marvelous creations in such a picture. The eyes of many men and women, who are authorities, have often lost the magic of imagination.

As we grow up we are trained to believe only in what is perceived with the physical senses. The ability to dream remains dormant and people limit their lives to what they can see, hear, taste, smell or touch physically. They put aside the beautiful world of illusion and fantasy where everything originates.

Many adults feel they are experts so they can train and correct children like Pedrito, and they practically force the kids to live in a narrow and limited world, in a world where you believe only in what you see. What happens when the kids start to grow up? What do people tell them? Do something useful! Stop wasting your time! Grow up! Don't you understand? Stop daydreaming! Wait until you see how life really is! Life is so hard!

Everything is created first in the mind, and we keep insisting that boys and girls quit using their imagination. We ask them to "pay attention", without realizing that they are paying attention to a bigger picture, not to the 5% that it is perceived by the physical senses. They ARE paying attention; they are seeing a world that you gave up long time ago.

We will never have an original of a song or a picture. The original is in the mind of the one who created it. We can have the first copy. Next time you find yourself telling a child to "pay attention", stop for a minute and you pay close attention to what he/she is doing and ask questions: Where are you traveling? What color is it? What do you see?

Allow them to dream, help them to see more that the 5% you are used to. Start making the difference in their lives and give them what you did not get.

When was the last time you daydreamed? Are you creating daily? Or are you just re-creating the same thing over and over?

During the seminar sessions we can detect those who stopped dreaming and spend the days reviewing the past, the pain, the frustration, the anger and the resentment over and over.

They stopped dreaming, quit creating a different present and conform to what they know.

TANGLE: I CAN'T CHANGE
CHANGE: I DECIDE TO CHANGE

TANGLE:

I CAN'T CHANGE

CHANGE:

I DECIDE TO CHANGE

The arguments people have to not change their lives are tied to their limited ideas, their ignorance. Some put aside that wall and go after new horizons. Others simply wait for somebody else to change, while judging and complaining because that is all they know. The decision is attached to the need to have different results. In order to change it is necessary to get educated, to investigate, to read, to take classes, to cultivate the place where the changes are made: the mind. Knowing how the mind works facilitates the changes.

The mind is divided into the conscious and the subconscious. Pay close attention to the difference between the two. The conscious mind is the part of the mind with which you can think. To think is to analyze, to take an idea and find out what works, what does not work, what can be learned and what you can do differently next time.

We can accept or reject an idea using the conscious mind; that is the part less used by people; "people rather die than think" said the British philosopher Bertrand Russell (18 May 1872 – 2 February 1970).

People think they think, but the only thing they do it is to go in circles repeating the same thing over and over again. That's the reason people are depressed and upset. They do not make decisions; they just keep repeating the same stories all the time: usually it is something that happened a long time ago. They play the victim role. Why do these things happen to me? Why did he/she do that to me? I do not deserve that! And on and on. Time passes, people get busy with life and when they remember what do they do? They go back to the same questions and complain. Why did this happen to me? Days, weeks, months and years later they continue with the same pain and resentment. How many of you have been playing the same mental CD in your head for years?

Rebecca was complaining about her husband's infidelity. They had been married for 15 years, and she insisted that she had forgiven him because of the kids, however the fights and arguments continued every day. Rebecca reminded him of his infidelity each time they had any little situation, even though the infidelity had happened 12 years before.

Despite the years –some people go in circles for 10, 15, 20 years-, the emotions persist. The reality is that this is not really thinking.

At an early age, when we start developing the ability to analyze, we are trained not to think but to obey. When the little one asks: Why is the sky blue? Why can't I put my fingers in the electrical outlet? Why do I have to wear that shirt? The answer they get from their parents is: Because it is! Because I said so! Stop asking and obey now! Don't be so stubborn! You are so nosy! The implication is that asking is bad, incorrect and inappropriate.

Instead of using the opportunity to teach them how to think, we use those moments to train them to be sheep: to follow, to comfort with no questions, to be submissive.

Pretty soon they learn that thinking is incorrect. And then, when they make a mistake, they get yelled at: "Why don't you think? When are you going to start to think?"

It is probable that they will commence to think when they are allowed to do it.

In the subconscious mind is the "magic wand or the genie of the lamp". It is the same no matter what you say to this genie. Whether you say, "I am stupid" or "How smart I am", "Everything I do goes wrong", "I have bad luck" or "I am convinced that everything is going to be all right", the answer will always be the same: "Your wish is my command".

Everything you think can become reality. The subconscious mind works 24 hours a day, 7 days a week. It controls our actions most of the time.

During stressful situations, the subconscious mind takes control, it is our automatic pilot. It does not differentiate between fantasy and reality. Have you ever dreamed of being chased or of falling into a hole and you wake up sweating, scared, nervous and with tachycardia? It was a dream, but your body reacted to the emotions that were produced. For the subconscious mind there is no difference. The subconscious accepts everything, absolutely all; it is the conscious mind which is the one capable of accepting or rejecting the idea.

Hector had been telling his wife he was going to paint the exterior of the house, however he gave all types of excuses not to start: it was too hot or too cold, there was no money, he was busy, it was too hard, it was too much work, he was tired. He was a participant in a Leadership program where he let us know the situation and the fact that this was not the first thing he had procrastinated due to his laziness. We challenged him to paint the exterior of the house over the weekend. Initially he became angry and refused to contemplate the possibility of doing it. However, while grumbling as he lay in bed, he realized this was a normal behavior for him; he usually found excuses to not do things. That weekend he painted the house by himself, and started to paint the inside too.

Henry Ford, visionary and pioneer of automotive industry, said: "Whether you think you can or you think you can't, you are right".

How does the subconscious mind work? The subconscious mind is the automatic pilot. Imagine you are traveling in an airplane. You go from Phoenix to Paris. The pilot programs the automatic pilot; he sets the coordinates for Paris. During the trip the airplane does not go in a straight line. There are factors that get the airplane off course. Let's suppose turbulence, or a storm gets the plane off its route. The automatic pilot detects the deviation. It immediately returns the airplane to its planned way according to the coordinates. During the route the plane diverts many times from its course, however it will end up in Paris.

What happens if in the middle of the trip I change my mind and decide I want to go to Hawaii instead? Can I get there in this plane? The answer is no, the plane is programmed to go to Paris. How could I get to Hawaii in this plane? You (or the pilot) will have to change the coordinates to match the new destination.

Well, the subconscious mind works that way. Our coordinates start to be set when we are in our mother's womb. The baby gets the genetic charge and sensations from the mom and people around her. When the baby is born his conditioning continues through his physical senses and his emotions. Each experience he has becomes part of the mental map that will direct his life.

The subconscious mind can be compared with a closet. The conscious mind is the guard and it stands at the entrance. It can decide what gets in and what does not get in to the closet. The closet does not have that ability. The problem is that the guardian remains distracted because it has many other things to manage. Imagine the guardian standing in front of the closet with the door open. Now visualize the guardian sleeping or distracted by other things. People pass by and when they see the guardian being inattentive, they start throwing everything that they do not want into the closet, for example, the anger, fear, pain, resentment, love, tolerance or intolerance, sadness, happiness, etc. As time passes the closet is crammed with stuff.

As we grow older, we put things in that closet without even noticing. We are unaware of what we are doing. The guardian gets more and more absent and absorbed by the daily survival, media, environment, weather, economic situation, politics and politicians, and it becomes oblivious. As you can deduct from this, the conscious has no idea what is in the closet.

Whatever is in our cluttered subconscious determines most of our actions, that is why we have the results we have and we do not understand what's going on. We say we want something and we get something different. We are trying to go to Hawaii in an airplane programmed to go to Paris.

Let's examine an example: domestic violence. Some of the coordinates a victim of domestic violence has are: "I do not deserve", "I am good for nothing", "I only learn by spanking", "Nobody loves me". These ideas —or coordinates- were put in a person's mind at a very early age. Sometimes as early as a fetus stage and the ideas continue during the first years of life. With these ideas programmed in his/her mind, the person starts to act in such a way that he/she attracts to his/her life an abusive partner. At some point in his/her life, due to family or friend's pressure or some other circumstances, he/she decided to leave the abuser. What happens? The alarm goes off; the automatic pilot detects the deviation and immediately works to make the proper corrections. Just as it happens when the airplane goes off its marked route and the automatic pilot returns the plane to its course. The person _in a great number of cases- returns to the "normal" situation of abuse. The job of the subconscious mind is to make sure that whatever is in there becomes a physical reality.

Margarita lived for 20 years in a domestic violence situation. Her husband hit her and also verbally abused her and the kids. She used to kick him out of the house, and he always came back apparently repentant –for a few days-. As the violence increased and she realized that he was being unfaithful, she left him on several occasions, but she always came back. The situation seemed different for a couple of weeks but then it went back to the old pattern. She tolerated the mistreatment because "she did not want her kids to grow up without a father"; however time passed and her children grew up and asked her to divorce their dad.

When she attended the seminar, she understood that she was repeating her mother's pattern. Her mom was physical and verbally abused by Margaritas' stepfather. There was also sexual abuse, not toward her, but to one of her sisters. She used to hear her sister scream for help, and all she could do was to cover her head with the blanket. The stepdad had threatened to kill her and her mom if she said anything. She obeyed because of her fear, and the stepfather constantly insulted her: "You are useless, and you are so ugly nobody is going to love you", "I have no clue why you were born, you are a nuisance, get out of here". He also used foul language to refer to her. The same words which years later her partner was using against her.

Margarita believed that her life was worthless; this idea was planted in her subconscious mind. The genie responded to these ideas, and she attracted to her life a partner who confirmed what she thought of herself at a subconscious level.

Fortunately for Margarita, as she looked inside and understood the origin of these ideas and how the mind works, her life turned around. She made substantial changes. She started to love herself instead of waiting for someone else to love her.

TANGLE: IT IS YOUR FAULT I FEEL BAD
CHANGE: I AM WELL, YOU ARE WELL

TANGLE:

IT'S YOUR FAULT I FEEL BAD

CHANGE:

I AM WELL, YOU ARE WELL

When you get out of the "comfort zone" —you realize that zone has not been as comfortable as you think, although it is the only one you know, and those who have shared that zone with you will get scared. They are going to feel the change like an earthquake. They have been there for a long time; they have also accepted the status quo. Even though it hurts they, too, know what to expect next.

If someone lives in domestic violence, for example, everybody knows that the partner comes "in a bad mood" screaming, insulting and hitting. They also know that after the fact he/she is going to repent and ask for forgiveness and this gives everyone hope that there will be a different tomorrow.

Marina used to come crying to our classes. She felt relief for herself by talking about how her husband mistreated her, didn't pay attention to her and how she was up to the nose in debts. She was convinced he was to blame for the financial situation because there wasn't enough to cover all expenses, and he was "so irresponsible" that he didn't even notice all she did to please him.

As she started working on herself, she realized she was responsible for her own results –this did not mean her husband did not have part of the responsibility- because she was waiting for the changes to occur miraculously without any effort on her part. She decided to begin taking time for herself: exercising, playing with her kids, and talking and going out with her friends instead of wasting her time fighting. She understood she was not going to be able to change her husband and stopped blaming him and concentrated on making her own changes.

Her husband had his own process, and even though he refused to accept help from us, the support came from other sources. He got a DUI and the ticket was very costly. He had to go to driving school, and he learned there how to handle his aggressiveness. He spent five times the cost of the seminar, however he learned.

Marina noticed she and her daughters felt better, and the family relationship commenced to improve.

The Universe moves constantly, it is impossible for anything to remain "just the same": life improves or deteriorates; we are moving forward or going backwards.

Before you point fingers, find out what's going on inside you. Remember, when you point with a pointer finger, three fingers are directed to you. Of course it is easier to criticize, point, judge and blame, you are used to doing it. To accept responsibility takes effort; if it were so simple anyone would do it. However, looking at the results of human kind, it is evident that most of everyone practices the law of less effort.

Just remember that what's on the line is YOUR LIFE.

TANGLE: I WIN, YOU LOSE
CHANGE: WE ALL WIN

TANGLE:

I WIN, YOU LOSE

CHANGE:

WE ALL WIN

To the sound of the mariachi, bongos, drums and melancholic violins, the idea of the victim is present in the musical themes that get to "the heart". These ideas makes songs like "I am a loser", "I have to lose" very popular.

Why is it so important to see life from the loser's perspective? There is a need to connect with the weak, the poor and the betrayed ones. The tendency to declare one's support of the loser comes hand in hand with the idea that every time someone wins, another one loses. People make comments such as: "Poor guy, he was so eager to do it, and that big one took advantage of him. That big guy is so abusive, of course he is bigger, stronger, and on top of that he has money and the other one has nothing, how could the poor guy possibly win?"

Instead of applauding the effort, he/she is criticized. People become suspicious of the way the person won: "Of course, she got the promotion because she sleeps with the boss", "He is where he is because he is a nephew of the owner", "He is useless but good to cheat", "Remember that if you don't cheat you won't win" are some of the comments made. The comments imply that to win you have to take advantage of others, to mislead, or to trick someone.

Competition brings rivalry, the need to demonstrate power over others and a struggle to destroy the weak. Competition comes from the Latin word "competere" which means "to come together", which in later Latin became "to strive together". This last meaning is the most common one among people. There are many people believing they are "losers", feeling that they have not "won" in life.

During one of the dynamics of a leadership workshop, while outside with nature in a beautiful snowy landscape, we asked the participants to form groups and made an original snowman. The result was fantastic and the creations were unique. Then we requested that each person form 10 snow balls. The following instructions were given: "The purpose is to protect your creation". In a matter of seconds a battle unleashed there and it ended up with the demolition of the snowmen while everybody laughed.

We asked them why they destroyed those beautiful creations if they had spent time and effort to build them. Some of the participants answered "You told us to attack the other team".

It was interesting to prove that the mental programming about competition is so strong and is linked to the desire to win no matter what. The task was to defend, and they attacked.

We proposed a new idea: WIN-WIN

What do you think when you see these words together? Some answer: "I win double", "I win totally, everything!", "I am the only winner, that's the only thing I care about".

What does it mean for you to say "win-win"?

The idea is that I win and you win.

What's the most important thing to have a win-win situation? "50/50" some answered. "To be even" others affirm.

"Win-win" means both parties are satisfied and it is not necessarily half and half. "Win-win" implies that nobody has to lose anything for someone else to win. You don't have to take anything from anyone, there is plenty for everyone. We both can have it all and be happy.

It is a concept that goes against the common belief of "win-lose". From when we were little, we got lessons on winning at any cost, and someone else had to lose. Every game, every place such as school or home directed you toward competition.

Siblings compete for their parents' love; students compete for the teacher's attention; employees compete for a promotion; sportsmen compete for high scores.

At the beginning of a basketball game the kids were nervous, but quickly they started to enjoy the game. However as the game progressed one of the parents of the losing team became tense, and every time a player missed a shot he yelled angrily. His energy spread out fast, and the children began to feel nervous again and became unhappy. At the end of the game their faces denoted pain.

Rafael was one of the players, who explained to his mom that when they stopped enjoying the game, he realized his team was losing something more important than the game: they were losing their spirit and joy.

The team had won some games but had "lost" more, and according to the standards of "competition" the team was a losing team. However, at the end of the season Rafael commented: "It is true that we all win. "Win-win" is possible. We have learned to enjoy the game, make friends and learn that the most important thing in life is not to be a champion by points won, but to be better beings each day. The real win is the learning". Rafael was 13 years old.

Many marriages, partnerships, friendships, families, societies get destroyed due to this "win-lose" idea. The future becomes uncertain. When you apply "WIN-WIN" the understanding, tolerance, harmony and joy return, with the certainty that the experiences obtained –independently of the score- are useful for the self-growth, and above all, the objective which is to BE A BETTER HUMAN BEING.

TANGLE: IF I GIVE TO YOU, I WILL END UP WITH NOTHING
CHANGE: WHEN I GIVE, I RECEIVE

TANGLE:

IF I GIVE TO YOU, I WILL HAVE NOTHING

CHANGE:

WHEN I GIVE, I RECIEVE

We learn to give by convenience, expecting something in return: "at least a thank you" people say. We get forced to say thank you in exchange for a gift, otherwise we enter the "rude" club. We are not saying that being grateful is bad or incorrect, not at all. Being grateful gives us the opportunity to value what we have, instead of concentrating on what's missing or feeling envy. The point is that we are forced instead of acting naturally.

We learn to give with conditions: to feel accepted, to receive love, to be approved. Children give spontaneously and freely, but they start very early to be trained in the art of giving while expecting something in exchange.

This paradigm is linked to the scarcity of certain thoughts with which we grew up. We will talk about them later. The scarcity is not limited only to money, but also to stinginess toward service, love and appreciation of others. Individuals inhibit themselves from words of affection, altruist actions, community service and the service to others without expecting anything in exchange.

People live looking for love but they create barriers because "they have been hurt so much". They give what they have: resentment, anger, frustration and fury. If you want love, give it and if you feel you don't have anything to give, look for help.

When Ignacio came to our weekly workshop, he shared that he was devastated because his girlfriend had ended the relationship, and he was "going mad" to the point that he quit his job because he was unable to concentrate. He was in a state of deep depression. He insisted he loved that woman too much and that he was willing to give his life for her; he was ready to change, to stop drinking so she would stay in the relationship. He bought expensive gifts for her, threw her a big birthday party. He invested time and money in the relationship, and all he got in return was a simple "thanks". This made him furious. When we asked him how much he loved himself, his answer was: "I do not know".

The truth is that if the person does not love him/herself, it is impossible to love someone else. Ignacio was looking for ways to fill his emptiness, demanding to be reciprocated in the same way. The girlfriend felt his insecurity and decided to stop the relationship. When we told him that she had just given him a wonderful gift, his face broke down. We explained to him that the rupture of the relationship had given him the opportunity to look for help, to work on himself to change his mental tangles, to heal the wounds of the resentment of his father's alcoholism, and his mother's submission to domestic violence, and the pain of other life experiences. Ignacio was repeating his parent's story. He was giving, expecting something in return.

To give is indispensable to letting go.

Most everyone assures that they know how to give; however, they tie an invisible cord and sometimes a very long one to what is given.

They are just doing a swap or an exchange. They give to receive something; and if they don't get it, they get upset.

Let's suppose that it is the birthday of someone special for you, and you spend a good amount of time and a considerable quantity of money to get him/her a unique present. You look everywhere; it takes several hours to be able to find it. Finally you got it. You have it on your hands and you are positive he/she is going to love it. You asked the sales person to wrap it in the best paper and write very heartfelt words on a card. You feel happy and proud when you hand him/her the gift; you know you have given an excellent one. The person thanks you for the nice gesture.

You find out some days later that she/he has given the present that you gave her with so much love, to another person! Which it means, your gift was given away. How do you feel?

Stop reading for a while and pay attention to your real feelings.

Write it down, give yourself the opportunity to feel, set aside the reasoning and logic, and just feel.

After you write it down, continue reading.

If the words you have are: anger, frustration, depression, sadness, fury, uncertainty, confusion or any other similar word, it means you don't know how to give.

There are no negative emotions associated to the fact that the present was given if you gave with the heart. It does not matter what the other person does with the gift, you gave it. If he/she keep it, put it in a closet, under the bed, donates it, exchanges it or even breaks it, it is her/his business, not yours. You gave it, and it is not yours anymore. Let it go.

But if the emotions are negative, even though you are sure you know how to give, the results show a different story. You tie up a cord, you are expecting something back.

Laura was going through a complicated situation because she could not find a job, and she commented she did not have friends. She had helped a lot of people when she was in a good job, and now that she needed them most, nobody lent her a hand. She was uncomfortable and feeling hurt and resented the people whom she supported before and now were not responding to her request.

"If I help you, you owe me one" is part of the conditioning, programs and mental tangles. We express it verbally at times; we learned that way. During these occasions, we say nothing but the commitment stays fixed someplace in our mind.

If we have the opportunity to serve it should be done from the heart, without expecting anything in return, absolutely nothing. Also, when we are in need, we shouldn't assume that someone needs to pay a debt that simply does not exist.

Let's talk about the opposite: to receive.

Think about this situation: some time ago you had a complicated incident and asked for help from a friend. She helped you with no hesitation at all and thanks to her generosity you were able to move forward. However, months after this, your friend has a serious problem and she needs your support. She asks you for help. Unfortunately, you are not in a position to help her and have to say "no". How do you feel? Do not analyze it, just open your heart and feel the emotions.

Write down the first emotions that come to mind.

If some of the emotions are guilt, -because you felt obligated- or discomfort with yourself, you don't know how to receive. You feel indebted and think you have to return the favor. You feel remorse because you "owe her something", since she helped you when you needed help the most.

To give and to receive are the same. Do you have difficulty receiving? Is it hard for you to ask for help; and if someone gives you something, do you feel uncomfortable? Since you do not know how to receive, and to receive and to give are the same, then you do not know how to give.

Mabel and Rene bought a precious toy car for their five year old son Francisco. He was the only child, so they wanted to give him the best. The boy was happy, played with the car, and gave his parents a hug and a kiss as a demonstration of gratitude. The euphoric time lasted less than two days.

Some friends of the family came for a visit with their three year old son Jesus. The boys played but at the end of the get together, when the visitors said good bye, Mabel and Rene noticed that Jesus had Francisco's new car in his hand. The guests asked the boy to leave the car where he found it because it was not his. Francisco spoke up naturally and said: "I gave it to him". Both couples felt uncomfortable, and they decided that the right thing to do was to return the car to the original owner.

The boys did not understand what was wrong. They wondered why was it bad to receive and to then give what they had received to another. Rene and Mabel explained to their son the fact that the car was expensive, and they had bought with love for him, and how important was to appreciate the gifts. The boy protested: "But my friend wanted it and I already had played with it. It was mine". The father also did his best to help Francisco to understand that it was not polite to ask for things. Rene insisted that the boy shouldn't have requested the toy. Francisco quickly explained: "He did not ask for it; he just said he liked it, and I gave it to him". The father's answer was: "That was too bad, you are ungrateful and I am sure Jesus' parents will teach him not to go places accepting everything that is given to him".

Francisco's parents took on their hands the mission to teach their son to see as bad something that is natural. The boys could not understand the logic; however they got the lesson: if you give you need to expect something in return, and if you receive then you are obligated to give something back. To give and to receive is bad, it gets you in trouble. That was the lesson.

To give means to let go. After you give it, it belongs to the other person so he/she can do what he/she pleases with it. The person can accept it, reject it, give it to another, or get rid of it. Who gave it, if he/she gave it well, should be indifferent to what happens after the gift is given.

It is the same when we receive. If we know how to receive, we do not feel indebted to the other person. We just gave the other the opportunity to experience giving.

The usual question parents ask is: How can I teach my child to be grateful?

The answer is simple: To be thankful does not mean to feel obligated or to compromise with someone.

If we understand the universal law of compensation, we do not have to worry. We can give and receive freely. Everything we put in the universe returns to us and in many cases it returns multiple times. As soon as I give, I am receiving. I put the universal energy in movement; there is no need to be concerned with what goes next. I just trust. I give and receive with love, humbleness and abundance. The universe responds.

We are not talking only of material things. We are considering all areas of our lives: to give time, love, tolerance, compassion, a hug, a smile.

It is important to understand another aspect of giving and receiving.

IF YOU GIVE, "with conditions attached", YOU ARE NOT GIVING, YOU ARE TAKING. I am referring to the act of doing for someone else what they can do for themselves, which thus makes them feel incapable. For example, when parents do everything for their kids without allowing them to learn, kids will grow up unable to take care of themselves, to become dependent. The correct word is DISABLE or CRIPPLE.

This generates resentment as a response.

Raquel commented in desperation that her son did not have any dreams (or goals), all he wanted to do was to sleep and eat. He had abandoned school. At home he demanded food and did not help with the chores. The young man was 20 years old.

Raquel explained that she had made sure he had had everything since he was little. She did not want him to suffer as "I did"; so she used to buy everything he wanted. She allowed him to do anything he wanted; his wishes were orders for her. She chose his clothes, toys, and friends. In a few words, she lived for him.

Raquel could not understand why her son resented that and was angry at her after all she had done.

The problem was precisely that. The message he got from her doing everything for him was "Poor boy, you are so weak I need to protect you, I do not trust you; you are unable to do anything so I'll do it for you". At a conscious level it was comfortable for him and he got used to receiving everything, but internally he resented that.

Even though Raquel felt she gave her son everything, she was taking away many things. She stole his opportunity for growth, learning, development and especially the belief in himself. Not allowing him to make mistakes prevented him from learning.

Think about how many times you are taking while believing you are giving.

To give with conditions attached or by disabling or crippling is to take away the ability of a person to do things for himself.

TANGLE: I SAY WHAT I FEEL
CHANGE: I THINK WHAT I SAY

TANGLE:

I SAY WHAT I FEEL

CHANGE:

I THINK WHAT I SAY

If people think what they said, the world would be mute.

The words we use daily while talking, singing, writing or conversing with ourselves, come from the ideas that are generated in the mind. They come from our interior. It is absurd when people say: "I did not mean that, it just came out". If it came out, it was because it was inside. No excuses.

Some people justify their lack of sensibility and tact by saying: "I am honest, I am not a hypocrite, and I say what I feel". Those people do not think about what they are expressing. They just let out all the pain, anger, fury and resentment toward others because they do not accept themselves. They spent their lives criticizing, pointing fingers, emphasizing the "defects" of others, because they do not understand that the Universe is a big mirror and they are looking at themselves and they cannot accept it.

They use strong phrases which in reality mean the opposite of what they are saying, for example:

WHAT THEY SAY	WHAT IS INSIDE
"I hate gossipers"	"I love gossiping"
"It is impossible to trust people"	"I do not trust myself"
"People are two faced"	"I am not honest"
"He has a high -handed attitude"	"I feel inferior"
"They do not listen to me"	"I am not a good listener"
"It is too expensive"	"I do not deserve it"

When we get annoyed by a specific characteristic of someone else, it could mean either of the two following things:

1. It is one of my weaknesses that I do not accept I have

2. It is a quality I would like to have and I envy

Rosa attended the seminar THE CHALLENGE OF CHANGING YOUR LIFE. She walked in with a negative, arrogant and confrontational attitude, affirming that she was right but her husband, children and even her friends were wrong, and she was going to prove it. Her language was very scornful toward everything and everybody. Instantly we detected her anger and pain. She kept her posture during many of the exercises and was absolutely sure of her opinion, until a point when she finally spoke up –for the first time in her life. She had been sexually abused as a child. Finally, the real Rosa came out, a sensible, loving, sweet woman, who had been using a tough mask in a quest to protect herself based on the interpretation she made of the events surrounding her.

She had promised herself nobody was ever going to touch her again. She was not going to allow a man to get close to her with "bad intentions", so she pushed them away with insults and beatings, including the man who later became her husband. Rosa saw the weaknesses of everybody around her, because she did not like herself. She was unable to see the beautiful human being that was hidden inside her for fear of being hurt again. Her decision was to throw the rock first before someone threw it at her —and she did it very well. She threw rocks with all of her strength to get her anger out, while all the while she was really destroying hers and her family's lives. Rosa continues with her personal development and is still learning. Her changes have been tremendous even though she still has many tangles to unravel and she holds onto them to justify herself —or, better said, to have an excuse-- to not move forward. The important thing now is that she knows the cause of her problem and has tools she can use to fix it.

Language transforms ideas. Words can build or destroy.

One of the ways to evade responsibility comes hand in hand with a word commonly used. We use the word SOMEONE instead of "I". The word SOMEONE indicates an unspecified or unknown person. In this way nobody assumes the responsibility or leadership.

We hear frequently expressions such as: "If someone would do it", "someone says", "someone thinks". When you change the word SOMEONE for I there is a huge difference. When you use "I" there is responsibility — which many do not want to take.

It is different when you say: "If I do it", "I say", "I think". Changing the language is a big step in transforming our actions. Using a language of responsibility and compromise instead of just leaving it up in the air gives ownership to a statement.

SOMEONE is too unspecific. NOBODY knows SOMEONE.

I am responsible for what I say and do. What would it happen if you started removing this word from your vocabulary? You would see how quickly your attitude would change.

There are other words that people use to avoid responsibility. Here is another idea we share with you to practice.

People find many excuses to not make decisions.

"I was going to do it, but …"

"I was about to make it, but …""I would have come earlier, but …"

"I wanted to, but …"

"I considered it, but …"

"I was ready to do it, but …"

The word BUT is used to justify the results. After BUT usually comes an excuse.

Review your daily vocabulary and pay attention to how many times you use the word BUT as a way to excuse your poor performance and justify your mediocrity.

Another common word is DIFFICULT.

"Life is difficult"

"This is too difficult to do"

"I try, but it is difficult"

Some people add the superlative VERY to make it more dramatic: "IT IS VERY DIFFICULT".

Remember Henry Ford's phrase: "If you think you can, or you think you can't, you are right".

One of the participants in the leadership program used to repeat constantly "IT IS IMPOSSIBLE". We discovered that this was one of the phrases she heard over and over again while growing up. Any time she wanted to do anything, her mother responded with: "It is impossible, we are poor", "Stop dreaming, that is impossible".

Her results were disastrous. She believed it was impossible "to have a good relationship, to educate children with love, to be happy, all because she was poor". She thought that way, she behaved that way and her results matched the belief.

Some TRY to make the changes. They are always trying to change and end up exhausted due to the effort, when in reality they do not move.

Do this: close this book that you are reading, and then think about trying to pick it up, but only think about it, Ok?

What happens when you only think about doing it? Of course, you do not pick it up. When you pick it up, it is because you stop thinking and just do it.

Stop thinking and just DO IT!

There are many words which limit you. They stop your actions because you believe them. If you make some changes in your vocabulary, you will gain huge steps toward your inner change, and your results will improve.

TANGLE: I STOP DREAMING AND BELIEVING
CHANGE: I DREAM TO BELIEVE AND CREATE

TANGLE:

I GAVE UP DREAMING AND BELEIVING

CAMBIO:

I DREAM TO BELIEVE AND TO CREATE

We were born free of thought and action, with an immense capacity for learning. How do we learn? Usually through our physical senses: taste, hearing, smell, sight and touch. However, we have higher faculties such as: memory, reasoning, will, intuition and imagination, which present us with enormous learning opportunities.

When we are little, we let imagination fly with an impressive easiness, and we are able to create fantastic stories with incredible characters. We can fly, transform into giants, and have superpowers. There have been cases where kids jump from a building with a towel or a sheet tied to their neck believing they can fly. After a spanking, they stop believing. However, some continue imagining and creating to the benefit of humanity in general. The Wright brothers, US aviation pioneers, proved to the world that a machine heavier than the air could fly and take human beings to conquer the air. Thanks to their imagination, their mechanic abilities and perseverance, and despite the constant mocking from people and the many failures, Orville and Wilbur made their dream come true.

However many stop dreaming because they believe the story: "Dreaming is for the rich", "Only fools dream", "Stop dreaming and start working, be real, life is cruel!"

The great innovators put aside these ideas and used their imaginations to create. Many investors laughed at Walt Disney. Some believed he had gone mad when he spoke about creating an amusement park with a city of the future, however when they saw the monorail, they were astounded. Disney said: "Do not sleep to rest, sleep to dream, because dreams can become real".

During a dynamic exercise we asked people to close their eyes and image being five years old. We encouraged them to remember the games they used to play, and asked what the most important thing was: the game or the toy? Some share the time when mom's crisping pan became trains, the container's lids transformed into race tracks, car wheels, pyramids, gold coins, etc. A towel or sheet became a house to play with the dolls. It became a magic carpet, or a cape to fly and travel outside the planet, or to walk on the moon and even to go through Saturn's rings and around Jupiter to explore other galaxies.

While doing this dynamic, some participants found themselves in the middle of pain remembering profoundly sad stories of the past. Some vowed not to remember anything; they were convinced their memories were bad. Even worse, they decided to forget consciously or subconsciously because the memory was too painful. However, the emotions were there inside the memory box.

Roberto started to cry during this dynamic. The weight of his seventy plus years showed when he declared with a shaky voice and tears: "I am a man with no dreams". He breathed deeply before continuing. "I stopped dreaming so long ago, I don't even remember anymore. I was always told to leave those stupidities to others, that dreaming was for the rich and we were poor. How dumb I was! I did not need any money to dream, I just realized that".

We told Roberto the same as we are telling you now: Dream, make your imagination fly so you can believe and create your own destiny, putting aside the type of life others designed for you.

You can block the facts, but the emotions are still inside you. These emotions show up during stressful situations, over and over again, creating addictions. Yes, we get addicted to anger, frustration, resentment and pain, which we experience while growing up.

We will talk more in detail about this in a later chapter.

Right now, give yourself the opportunity to be a child again, remember those beautiful times when you dreamed, believed and created.

Allow that little one that is inside you to come out. It is time to heal the wounds of the past so you can live with intensity and plenitude.

It is time to dream and imagine. Einstein said: "Imagination is more important than knowledge". He was right.

Decide to dream again.

TANGLE: I WEAR MASKS TO HIDE
CHANGE: I TAKE OFF MY MASK TO BE HAPPY

TANGLE:
I WEAR MASKS TO HIDE

CHANGE:
I TAKE OFF MASKS TO BE HAPPY

Every day we have opportunities to learn, to unlearn and to re-learn. Each experience is an opportunity to test our abilities. However, when a frustrating situation occurs, the tendency is to adopt a behavior to end the circumstance that is uncomfortable. The mechanisms are automatic and they have the goal to protect us from pain, tension or any other negative emotion produced by the situation.

It is important to give yourself the chance to open your mind and your heart to do your personal growth work, even when what you see inside you is unpleasant.

The work is to look inside and when something we see is uncomfortable, automatically we start to use a defense mechanism such as: repression, negation, rationalization, internalization, regression, displacement and sublimation.

We won't get into the details of these mechanisms, since we are not writing a psychology book. Our objective is to share the knowledge in an agile, simple and effective manner.

It happens frequently that people commence to use these mechanisms because the new ideas make them feel uncomfortable. Some of the reactions are the following:

- Anger

They throw tantrums and block the chance to change because they are upset, according to them, with the new ideas. Pretty soon they realize that the anger is with themselves.

- Crying

They cry to cause pity, because their life stories are "so hard" that nobody understands them. They feel victims of the circumstances and use the tears to gain sympathy. It is a good excuse to not do what they need to do. It is important to add that the tears have another important function: it is to cleanse and heal. Men should give themselves the opportunity to cry so they can remove those tangles like "men do not cry, the ones who do are gay or girls".

- Repression

They keep their emotions for fear to appear vulnerable or to be judged. They wear masks of insensibility and/or toughness.

- Laughter

They ridicule others and themselves through jokes and stories to get attention on the outside instead of on the inside.

- Isolation

They look for ways to separate the memories from the feelings and pretend not to feel anything. At times they enclose themselves in a profound silence and do their best to hide in a "small box" so nobody can see them.

- Ignoring

They do not follow the commands or homework; they stop paying attention and assume closed body postures.

- Judging and criticizing

They take a specific point of view from their perspective and interpretation, and express their judgments with negative comments about others and thus take control.

- Displacement

They channel their feelings toward someone else. For example, they get upset with us because we represent the authority figures such as father and mother. They usually get even with the family, the partner, or their kids, blaming them for the situation.

- Negation

They ignore the reality, pretending it does not exist. They invent stories to compensate for the pain and believe them.

- Talking without stopping

They have the answer for everything and everybody, and they share it at all times; they give advice, to fix others' lives even though theirs are a mess.

- Projection

They feel the painful emotions or ideas are not theirs, they belong to someone else. They point fingers.

- Introjection

The person incorporates subjective features that belong to

others; they feel empathy and share others' pain, they feel it as if it were theirs; they even get mad for the situation of the other person and defend them as though it were personal.

Some people respond with anxiety, depression and biological dysfunctions like: getting hungry or losing their appetite, getting insomnia, having a stomachache, itching in different parts of the body. Often they can't stand to be in one place and move from place to place. Some of them go to the bathroom continuously.

Sebastian got up every 20 minutes and went to the bathroom, stayed there for a while and then he came back to the room. When we explained the different avoidance mechanisms, he realized that his kidney problem was just an excuse to not look inside himself. He remembered that when he was little he used to hide in the bathroom to avoid being smacked by his dad and to avoid seeing the beatings his mom and siblings got from his dad. From that moment on, he was conscious of the situation, the trips to the bathroom decreased until the point where he was able to wait until the break to go.

The ways to avoid reality go together with different body postures, generally closed ones: arms and legs crossed, hands in the pockets, feet under the chair, fingers interlaced, sluggish –posture of "whatever"-, head down. People also use accessories such as hats, eye shadow, caps and tend to dress in black. Black is an elegant color, but it is too a way to mark a divisive line so others do not get close. It is distant and somber.

Mario is a heavily built guy, who came with an expression that read "do not get near me". He hid himself under the hood of his sweater, kept his hands in the pockets, dressed in black except for his bright red tennis shoes. Under the sad face there was a sweet and gentle but angry kid. He never met his dad, lived in extreme poverty, and on many occasions he had to eat the waste found in the dumpsters. He grew up with insecurity, holding onto his mom, who used to ridicule him in front of others because that was the only way she knew to educate him to be a good man. Mario dressed in black for two days. The third day, after he freed himself of the heavy loads of the past, he showed up with an orange T-shirt, green-lemon sweat pants and, of course, his bright red tennis shoes. A wonderful promoter, he danced, laughed and learned to give energetic hugs, something he had been formerly prohibited to do because it was "dirty" and "indecent" and people "might think badly about him".

Mario learned to assume responsibility for his actions, changed his vocabulary, and started to say "I love you" to his children; he reintegrated with his family and began to take initiative instead of waiting for someone to tell him what to do. He stopped isolating himself and modified his wardrobe by introducing the colors he really liked and which made him feel great.

He ceased to use defense mechanisms and opened to the opportunity for change. Others from the group detected his mechanisms and help him by letting him know he was changing.

It is interesting that others can see when you are avoiding, but you can't. The tendency is to say: How come he doesn't notice? "Doesn't he see what he is doing and what they are telling him is true?" There is a big temptation to speak for others. On many occasions some people find the solution for the neighbor's problem but not for their own. Of course, we are not talking about you, you are different and maybe you are the type that when finding out there is a seminar where you can work on yourself to improve as a human being, said something like: "I am fine, I do not need that. My wife or husband, children, friend, sibling need it", "That's for mad people and I am not crazy", "I can do it alone", "I am fine the way I am: why should I change?"

If you can respond with honesty in an affirmative way to the question "Are you completely happy?" Then keep doing what you are doing, and look for options to continue learning, you are on the right path; it is a daily goal to look inside and share your happiness.

However if the answer is negative or you say things like: "It is impossible to be happy at all times", "I would be happy if I had money", "When the economy improves, I will be happy", "I want my children to be happy, even if I am not", then you need help.

Where do children learn to be happy or to have healthy relationships, to trust, to be leaders, to forgive?

We are the mirror where they reflect themselves; they learn from what they see, hear, and feel at home. What inheritance do you want to leave for them?

The first step is to decide to make the changes. It is like cleaning a closet. We know it smells bad. Every time we get close, or someone opens the door a little bit, the smell gets to us and immediately we pretend that there is no smell or blame the neighbor. We convince ourselves that it is the neighbor's closet which is the stinky one.

We won't be able to clean it until we change our mind. Then we need the courage to face the truth. We must accept that the smell comes from our own closet, and then we can start checking it out. During the review process we will be tempted to close it again and pretend nothing happened; we will blame, judge, fight, avoid, deny, and criticize because that is what we have learned since we were little.

You are not your past, but the decisions you make now must be in the present and with a new perspective.

TANGLE: LIFE TREATS ME BADLY
CHANGE: I TREAT LIFE FAIRLY

TANGLE:
LIFE TREATS ME BAD

CHANGE:
I TREAT LIFE FAIRLY

We weave tangles at the least provocation. As soon as we are under stress we bring up painful stories of the past.

Many people see themselves as calm, serene and assured us that they live in peace, but they clarify that if someone "gets them mad", "THEY DO NOT HAVE ANY CONTROL". They can insult, swear and even start looking like the green character "Hulk".

To be calm when everything goes right has no merit. To maintain your peace in moments of stress is a challenge.

Your character is tested during difficult situations. If there is a tendency to explode, it is just a matter of time, because the pressure has been building inside. If the answer to a provocation is calmness and serenity, then you truly have inner peace.

Our level of tolerance is measured with each of our actions, or better said the way we react or respond.

A simple way to measure it is by the way you drive. Imagine yourself behind a steering wheel waiting for the stop light to change. You are distracted listening to music when the green light goes on and half a second later, the driver behind you sounds the horn repeatedly to make you move. You look through your rear mirror and what do you do?

1. Do you get your hand through the window and give him a finger?

2. Do you curse and insult him?

3. Do you stay there without moving on purpose?

4. Do you continue calmly to the speed limit?

5. Or, you image the person has an emergency or maybe he/she needs to get to the bathroom quickly!

Which are the stories you make up? Do you make them up with anger and then figure out excuses to justify your bad temper saying: "Everything was going smoothly until that guy made me mad".

WELCOME TO YOUR LIFE.

The way you react to situations that are out of your control, indicates the usual way you behave in life.

You can waste your time looking for culprits and pointing fingers, however every time you aim your pointer finger at someone, three fingers are pointing back at you. Remember if it came out, it is because it was inside you.

Next time you are driving, remember this exercise.

There are many other ideas that come out of you, such as: when you compare yourself with the "beautiful arrogant girl who's driving a convertible next to you". You think: "Most likely she is going out with a politician or a drug dealer", or _if it is a gentleman- "I want one like that to show off to my friends".

Think of all the other ideas that come to your mind.

Mirna was at a restaurant with her family, her husband and the in-laws, the waiter came with the drinks but lost his balance. The lemonades and a beer fell over Humberto, Mirna's husband. Humberto had some options when faced with the surprising shower that left him soaking wet: He could have

1. Got upset and shouted at the waiter for the reckless

2. Exited the site to show his discomfort - which would have terminated the family dinner

3. Demanded an apology, ask not to be charged a penny for the dinner of ten.

4. Talked to the manager and emphasized the inadequacy of the waiter.

His decision was to stay despite:

Despite being soaked from back to toe

Despite smelling of beer and lemonade

Despite the cold bath from the ices

Despite the laughter and amazement of the audience

Despite the jokes that came after

He dried himself with a towel and jokingly asked for his drink again. The evening passed pleasantly.

We have seen how some people are upset because the waiter served a wrong dish, or when the steak is not cooked correctly. . Many diners assume attitudes of arrogance, as if the world owes them something, and angrily criticize the service —some do it on purpose to not pay the bill, but that's another story.

How Humberto reacted to an unexpected situation, reflects his inner state of inner peace, one of the multiple reasons Mirna loves and admires her husband.

Practice this exercise:

Imagine you are in a conference room with 20 coworkers and the facilitator asks everyone to take a blank sheet and have a pen on hand.

Everyone is told that they have two minutes to write his/her name as many times as possible. Then the speaker begins to count backwards and aloud.

What do you do?

You wonder if it was with the two names, or just a first name? Do you start writing quickly, trying to beat your friends? Turn your eyes to see the paper of one of them, seeing how they do for it? Copying ideas? Many may have doubts, but you would rather stay silent for fear of being laughed at because you are the only one who did not understand the instructions? The clock is ticking and there is one minute left. Do you keep writing equally in each line? Do you follow a pattern or make changes along the way?

You feel that this is a competition, not only against the clock, but with your coworkers, so you have to prove you're the best, you will finish first and you confirm that you are efficient and that way you win their respect; or think it makes no sense anyway to hurry since you never win anything, you just do what is your job, after all no one recognizes your effort.

Think about the ideas flooding your mind from a simple instruction. Because the way you react to that idea, is a reflection of what you do every day.

Analyze whether these ideas contribute to building a successful and happy present in your life, or if instead the ideas negatively impact your results.

The decision to change is always within you.

TANGLE: I AM STUCK
CHANGE: I MOVE FORWARD OR BACKWARDS

TANGLE:
I AM STUCK

CHANGE:
I MOVE FORWARD OR BACKWARDS

When you greet people and ask them: How are you? many respond "the same", "nothing different", "just doing", "nothing new", "as bad as yesterday". It's actually impossible to be the same since we change daily, the Universe is constantly changing and we, as part of the Universe, change too.

In life there are two options: go forward or go backwards. The "status quo", the state of things at one time, is an illusion, it is a lie; it does not exist. The universe is moving all the time, it is dynamic. If you say "I am the same", actually what happens is that you are going backwards and have not noticed. Possibly you are a little frustrated, angrier, madder and sadder. What's going on with you? If you are not taking risks, you are not learning and therefore going backwards. If day in and day out you do the same, in the same way and with the same energy, it means you have stopped growing, making mistakes and therefore not learning. If you don't advance, you go back.

When you feel very comfortable, you are in a dangerous zone. Comfort is perhaps one of the most dangerous conditions in the world.

Raul spoke with us about how comfortable he was feeling, "All is fine. Every day is the same. I get up at the same time, I go to work. I know exactly what they expect from me at work and I know how to do it because it's the same every day. I return home to my children, as always, this is routine. It seems that nothing changes in my life, everything stays the same".

We asked him if he was sure that everything was the same, and we clarified that if progress was not made it means deterioration was happening. His answer was short and direct: "I am fine the way I am now, I do not think I need to do something different".

A few months later he came back worried and having serious difficulties with his children. According to him, everything was perfect and problems arose suddenly. In assessing the situation he realized that the children were showing changes and he refused to accept them. It was more comfortable to think that all was well. He had ignored the symptoms. While assuring that all was well, actually his family relations deteriorated.

Often this situation is seen in couples. Marcela was in shock because her husband filed for divorce. He explained he was in love with another woman. Marcela insisted on the fact that their relationship was fine, everything was the same; nothing had changed between them, and that they had been several years together. Actually communication between the two deteriorated gradually. What she viewed as "the same" was her denial of the fact that the relationship was moving backwards.

Advance or regress. The fastest way to go back is to pretend everything is the same.

We go backwards when we fail to take risks, to live life as we want to live, or when we insist that others live their lives the way we want to live, when we want to control everybody else, when we stop learning, when we allow the fear to control our lives, when we live in the past or in the future while ignoring the present.

We cease to move forward if we are full of hatred, anger, resentment, pain, and sadness. These are heavy burdens that prevent us from moving.

We start to move forward when we risk, when we are wrong and learn from those mistakes, when we live our lives as we want and we have faith in God, in ourselves and in others. We continue progressing when we decide to take control of our lives, be responsible. And finally we can move forward by leaps and bounds when we forgive. Releasing the hatred, fear, ignorance, anger and sadness, we feel lighter and can move quickly.

To advance is important to live well in the present. We learn from the past and expect for the future, however, we really live in the present.

Use past experiences as learning tools and focus in the present to design the future you want.

What would happen if you left a fruit on top of your kitchen table for several days? Depending on the weather, it would completely dry or rot. In any weather, it would deteriorate.

What would it happen to your muscles if you did not exercise them? They would lose tone, strength, flexibility and atrophy.

If you do not make decisions but you allow others to decide for you, you will get depressed, you will get frustrated, you will deteriorate, and you will go backwards.

Do you want to continue learning to advance or are you already going backwards in your life?

You have the steering wheel, the control of your vehicle, which will take you wherever you want to go. Decide.

TANGLE: I HEAR YOU
CHANGE: I LISTEN WITHOUT TALKING

TANGLE:

I HEAR YOU

CHANGE:

I LISTEN WITHOUT TALKING

The main complaints between parents and children, couples and businesses, are due to communication problems.

Communicating is straight-forward: the sender sends a message through a channel and the message reaches a receiver. Easy, right?

Problems arise by the way we communicate. Remember that the issuer, who originates the message, has his own values, frameworks, interpretations, life history, etc. But, he is "supposed" to be sending the message with clarity, sharpness and precision so that the other person MUST understand correctly.

During the process, other factors also produce as much noise in the environment and in the channel. If you add to this that the receiver has its own values, frameworks, interpretations, life history, etc.., the results will not be very encouraging.

The simplest example is the game of "Broken Telephone", where a message is passed directly into the ear of a participant, who in turn shares it with someone else, and this person with another and so on. When the last person expresses aloud the message you first received, it will not resemble the original, because everyone has added or taken away according to their own perception and interpretation.

We also have to bear in mind that hearing is not the same as listening. When listening, we pay attention.

It is common to hear the complaint of young people who say their parents do not understand them. A mother usually does not stop washing dishes, sweeping, mopping, and cooking, while her son wants to communicate his concerns, desires, or just share with her a daily event. If the young man says: "You're not paying attention", the mother might reply: "I have many things pending, and oh yes, keep talking"; the same often happens when Dad takes over the TV remote. The children want to share something with him, but the dad's eyes are glued to the screen —especially if it is a sport event. Then parents complain that their children do not ask their opinion. Actually, since there has been no focus on the conversations; the parents hear only part of what the child is trying to communicate. And later, the parents are upset because the child does not quit watching TV or playing computer and video games, when the parent is trying to say something.

Women have similar complaints about their husbands: "He loves the TV more than me "," He does not touch me as he does the remote control", "He just pay attention to the TV, how is he going to listen to me?"

Have you ever thought about how you listen? Do you really listen or do you just give the appearance that you are listening?"

In simple terms we can say that there are three common ways which people listen:

1. Agreeing with

   Recall a time when your friend was telling you a story and automatically you remembered a similar one that happened to you. Before the other person finished talking, you interrupted to share your story, and then your friend took advantage of a moment you stopped to breathed to continue his own story once again. This conversation, if you can call it that, may continue for hours both speaking and not hearing the other; each focused on his own story.

2. Disagreeing with

   This form of listening is very common among adolescents and their parents or between couples. When the person is talking, the other party is putting together an argument to prove the other is wrong as soon as he has the opportunity to begin to fight back. Each focuses on proving that he is right and the other wrong. Usually no one is allowed to finish his sentence or to counter-attack. In couples this often happens. One of them is talking and as soon as the other closes his mouth, or even before, the other begins to give arguments.

   Meanwhile, young people are ready to prove that their dads and moms are outdated, and the parents are ready to prove that the children are the ones who are wrong. As a result they end up upset and the generation gap opens more and more.

   In these two ways of listening, the conversation becomes two monologues that occur simultaneously. No person is actually listening to the other and therefore there is no communication.

3. Being with

   This way of listening allows real communication. Just being with the person.

How do you know that someone is really listening to you? What are the signs that show you that she/he is listening?

Both people make eye contact; they both look at each other's eyes and maintain an open body position, i.e., arms uncrossed, hands-free, and the body closer to the other person, without invading their living space. These are clear signs that the person is alert and focused on listening.

Imagine for a moment the changes in your personal relationships if you would often stop to listen this way.

Gabriel and Encarnacion came to one of our workshops and stayed at the end to talk to us. Gabriel told us that his wife did not speak, did not express her feelings. While she wept silently, always with her head down, her partner talked and talked about her.

We allowed him to let off steam and then laughingly said: Right, she does not speak. How will she if you never shut up? Can you have a few minutes of silence, to allow her to express herself? He looked surprised and stopped. Gradually Encarnacion said she felt intimidated, because every time she wanted to say something, she was interrupted. She even received insults for speaking at low volume and not being able to communicate what she wanted to say. She was so scared that she could not speak, so we decided it was better to leave it that way for a moment to avoid arguments. Both started doing personal development work through the programs we teach and Encarnacion today has found her voice and her husband has learned to listen.

Gradually relationships are destroyed for lack of communication, by not listening with the heart and mind.

If we learn to listen, without criticism, without judgment, without feeling offended, without taking everything as a personal attack, we would have extraordinary relationships.

Surely many times you have found yourself in a situation where your child, your spouse, or friend insists that they told you something and you are convinced that never happened. Or simply do not remember. The reality is that you do not remember because you never heard it. You were so busy waiting for your turn to talk that the other person's words became only a murmur.

Often people say, "I have a bad memory for names, I was just introduced to that person and I do not remember his name." The real situation is that you did not hear the name, because you were waiting for your turn to tell yours. If you listened carefully then you'd remember. Practice listening to your partner, your children and friends with the third type of listening … "being with".

When someone says: "I want to discuss something with you", stop what you're doing, stop for a moment, look him in the eyes and listen. Ask questions about what they are sharing and avoid telling your own story at that time.

If your partner or children want to talk to you, show them how important they are to you. Turn off the TV, computer, cell phone, and place yourself in a position to send the message "I hear you, I'm with you, I'm interested in what you want to share with me."

If you apply this, you will find that your results change.

Communicating from the heart is natural but not always the norm. The child says everything he thinks and feels. The child does not care if someone is upset or offended by what he has to say. He is honest, sincere, and spontaneous.

Martha was invited to a dinner at a friend's house and she decided to take her little brother. Dinner was delicious, everything was going very well until the end of the meal when Martha turned to the boy and said: "What do you say?" He quickly and loudly said: "I am still hungry." Martha felt extremely embarrassed. She hoped that her brother would say "Thank you". The hostess quickly rectified the situation by bringing the child another meal. However, on the way home, Martha scolded her brother and reprimanded him for the inappropriate comments. He still did not understand. "I was hungry," the boy insisted. "Was I supposed to lie?"

During the period of "domestication", we are taught to stop being natural to enter the world of "normal or accepted social behaviors". Don Miguel Ruiz affirms that there comes a time when we are so domesticated, we do not need anyone else to domesticate us, because we become our own self-tamer and domesticate ourselves according to the belief system we have received and by using the same punishment and reward system which we have learned. We pass on these traits to our children, without question, because it was taught to us, even if we disagree or have doubts.

While teaching a workshop in an elementary school, and sharing these ideas about domestication and mental programming, a mother commented that one day her five year old son broke a glass. Before she could react, the little boy approached her with a belt while saying: "Here, hit me because it's the only way I learn."

We learn from our childhood that normal means what is common to most people, no matter that the behavior has no reason or sense, no matter that it violates core values. It is normal to criticize, judge, point fingers, beat, insult, ignore, to have daily monologues with our loved ones, pretend that we hear when all we are doing is waiting for our turn to speak. It is normal to judge the opinion of others and insist that ours is the only one that counts, or to pretend that our emotions are normal and to be offended when others express theirs.

Communicating from the heart with the truth of course is natural. We forget as we grow. We built a wall around us and begin to forget who we are and what we really feel. Most people have superficial relationships, talk about everyone, but do not express what they really feel.

They base their comments on stereotypes that have been created mentally. They justify and defend their positions, because they are theirs!

Often people come to the office and tell us about the difficulties they are facing with their trading partners. They are about to end the relationship and take their own path, while insisting that the other one is wrong.

Juan came seeking support to improve the relationship with his wife and also told us he was about to dissolve his business partnership. He said he put in one hundred percent at work, doing his part. During the conversation he also told us he was looking for a part time job because he could not survive with what he earned in his company. "Are you sure you give 100 percent?" we asked him, and he emphatically said, "Yes!" The numbers did not add up. He was upset because his partner had another job and therefore a guaranteed salary while he did not, so it was not "fair".

Any question we asked, he gave a pretext, an excuse not to face the fact that he was ready to defend himself. He spoke at level 2, the "disagreeing with" level. When at that level of communication it is very difficult to reach an understanding. The interesting thing is that the same thing had happened in his marriage. That was a reason he was about to divorce.

To develop lasting relationships it is necessary that both people are willing to take off the mask, open their hearts and take risks.

The first time Clara and Mirna had a telephone conversation both had a warm feeling. It's easy to feel a genuine human being. They talked on several occasions and a few months later had the opportunity to start their partnership, which they named AVANTE seminars "Training for Life". It was in July 2008 and in August they were offering their first seminar, which lasted four days. Several people asked how long they had run the company and were highly surprised when the women replied that it was the first seminar together and that they had met only a few months ago. "It seems that you had known each other for many years," people said. Both of them also felt as if they had known each other for a long time.

The success in their business relationship which has also impacted their emotional development, is that above their partnership, they are friends, and have implemented LISTEN by "being with", to connect the mind with the heart; even when they disagree, they listen at level 3, without criticizing and judging, understanding that they are different and process ideas differently, too.

They always try to listen without speaking, and laugh a lot, which gives flavor to the friendship and working relationship.

TANGLE: WHAT A FOOL I AM
CHANGE: I AM PROUD

TANGLE:
I'M SUCH A FAILURE

CHANGE:
I FEEL PROUD OF MYSELF

Some people are so used to seeing the negative side that it is very easy for them to judge others. They do not realize that by doing so, they judge themselves because the universe is a mirror, and we receive back everything we send.

Failure to recognize the virtues and benefits of those around us means we have failed to accept ourselves as the wonderful beings we are. What we do not like in others, we do not like in ourselves, and we project the discomfort to others because we have trouble recognizing our mistakes.

Karen, one of the young people who participated in several of our self-development programs, said during one of the meetings that she did not know that "gossiping" was bad, because at home everyone talked about others, and of course criticized, judged and prosecuted everyone. For her gossiping was normal because she had grown up in a home where gossip was part of family life. It was also very interesting to see that exceedingly judgmental and gossipy people bothered her. The displeasure make her fight with them, answer them emphatically and in a quite bigoted manner in situations where people spoke ill of her friends. But she did not walk away from the place because there she found things she did not hear elsewhere. Besides she took advantage of those moments to criticize and even imitate body movements to mock others.

Karen had not realized that other people were her reflection. What bothered her so much about others was exactly what she did, but could not see herself. That is, Karen was not aware of her actions; she could only distinguish them in others.

For some people it is easier to judge because they do not accept themselves. It is easier to detect a "defect" than a quality. They are so used to it that they have trouble thinking of something good in others and in themselves. The main reason is that they do not know how to forgive and are not able to forgive themselves. The habit of ill-treatment has become so ingrained that even to themselves they say aloud: "I am so stupid", "What a moron, I made a mistake again", "I am so dumb", "I am more stupid each day, my mother was right", "Maybe I need some bangs with a stick to see if I learn", and some other stronger phrases. These are the same phrases they were told over and over again; they accepted them, believed them and acted accordingly. This is the reason it is so hard for them to recognize the good qualities and instead only distinguish the weaknesses in themselves and in others.

Isabel is a close friend and was very dismayed when she was told her ex-husband was in critical condition in the hospital; he was terminal. Although they had divorced sourly many years ago, had fathered two children together and were almost adults, I detected much confusion about their relationship during my conversation with Isabel, while we talked through internet chat. She claimed that there was no resentment that she already had forgiven him for everything that had happened between them, that she had already said what she had to say and that she was in peace. But when I asked her to write 10 qualities of her former partner, she took a couple of minutes thinking, then wrote five and stopped there. "I can't find more" she wrote in chat. I asked her to seek others and then she wrote: "He was not a good father, not a good provider, and he was not affectionate." I asked her to stop, because those were not qualities but part of the resentment she had towards him and towards herself for having supported that relationship of many years.

One of the most effective tests to see if you have truly forgiven is that you can talk about the situation without pain and if you can extol the qualities of the person or persons who "apparently" offended you.

And one of the first steps that we invite you to take is to make a list of 100 qualities you have. You might think that it is too many, that you do not have all those, you've suffered a lot, that your life has been so hard and only bitterness is in it and cannot see anything good in you.

Guilt and resentment prevent you from seeing all those moments where you felt proud of yourself.

Mind you, this is not to speak of the merits of your children or your parents. This is to acknowledge your greatness through the many occasions when you feel the adrenaline in your body; the endorphins that make you feel happy for the courage of your actions.

Today you have a great opportunity to start communicating with the heart. For a long time, you have worn armor, pretending to be what you are not for fear that others can see who you really are. It's time you started to let out that wonderful person inside and start to shine, to get the light that is within you, to enlighten your life and help to illuminate the way for others.

When you finish the list of 100 qualities, read it again and again. If there is something that stirs within, if you start to weave stories and build tangles that "I'm not so good" "That was me before but not now," and so on, remember that the most important thing is that you BELIEVE it. What others believe about you, is their business. The most important thing is what you think of yourself.

If you think you are "stupid, useless, good for nothing", the subconscious, the genie, says you're absolutely right.

So it's time to start feeling proud of yourself, your goals, your small and great triumphs; be proud of everything you've accomplished to reach the place where you are now. When you accept your greatness, you will see the greatness in people around you, because they too have triumphs and failures and are proud of what they have accomplished. Recognize their virtues, honor their qualities, and express them aloud for the echo of your words resonates within you. Get to see the wonderful being you are so you can it in others. They are your reflection.

TANGLE: I WANT YOU TO UNDERSTAND ME
CHANGE: I WANT TO UNDERSTAND OTHERS

TANGLE:
I WANT TO BE UNDERSTOOD

CHANGE:
I WANT TO UNDERSTAND OTHERS

We are the result of the seeds that others have put in us. It is our responsibility to help them germinate to reap the rewards. No one has been done and polished alone. We learn from each experience and we make decisions based on these experiences.

Human behavior has been evaluated from multiple perspectives. For the purpose of our work in AVANTE SEMINARS, we have combined some ideas to help the people to know themselves, and know others, with the aim of improving their relationships. The way we behave largely determines our results. This influences the temperament and character that define the personality. Temperament is the natural way in which a human being interacts with the environment and may be hereditary. The character is molded through the intellect and will, in addition to the great influence of the environment.

The first systematized the idea of temperament was the Greek physician Hippocrates (460-370 BC), who distinguished four types, considered as an emanation of the soul by the interrelations between different humors in the body:

- Choleric, irate, people whose humor is characterized by a strong will and some impulsive feelings, dominated by yellow and white bile.

- Phlegmatic, people that are delayed in the decision-making, they tend to be apathetic, sometimes with much cold blood in them. The phlegm is the dominant component of the humors of the body.

- Sanguine, people with a very variable humor, snatched and disorderly.

- Melancholic, sad and dreamer people, who are easily influenced.

After this first attempt to systematize temperament, changes have been made. There are different theories and today some of them have been made popular.

Although initially the division which distinguished types of temperament or personality, it is accepted today that the differences are of behavior or mood rather than personality. These are ways in which we react or respond to the circumstances of our daily lives, especially those of stress.

There are people who are regarded as formal, others are informal, some let themselves be influenced by others, are tolerable, and some more are dominant.

Observe the following graph with the division of the forms of behavior in four major areas: drivers or controllers, analysts, promoters and supporters.

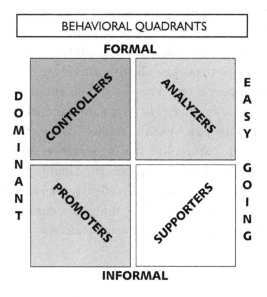

Some characteristics of each group are:

- Controllers

    Dominant, they don't hear reasons, they want to impose decisions, are individualistic, determined, bold, intolerant and impatient. They want all in perfect order and send others to do it well and fast. If they can't find whom to order they get angry, explode, shout and blame others of the results when the results are not satisfactory. If the result is good, they are left with all the credit. They are perfectionists, save rancor with ease, injure others and rarely apologize. They have no problem with conflicts, they need freedom to manage others and themselves, do not show their emotions, are independent, pretend to be insensitive; they are impatient, bad-tempered, energetic, ambitious, passionate, efficient and competitive.

- Analysts

    Tolerable, followers, they take their time, struggling to decide because they continue to analyze every detail, speak slowly and in a low voice, are simple, give many explanations, justify themselves, follow methods to carry out their activities, do not skip any step, prefer quiet environments where they can learn, and are isolated from people. They are skilled in areas of analysis and numerical operations. They keep their emotions to themselves and are very sensitive. They are cautious, melancholic, remain trapped in the past, -like the "oldies" songs - they like to get in contact with nature, like the organization and structure, ask questions, they tend to be pessimistic, highly creative in poetry and art, rely on the data and statistics, prefer intellectual work, they enjoy being in the right thing, are careful with the time and money, work slowly and usually alone.

- Promoters

Dominant, leaders of parties and social events, fearless, determined, have a great tendency to enjoy adventure, launch jobs without planning, say yes to everything that sounds fun, never discuss, do not take life so seriously, enjoy each moment, are cheerful and infect others with joy, reach their goals – sometimes unaware of how they did it - and they rejoice. They get motivated by recognition, acceptance and contact with people. Usually they give a good impression, verbalize, motivate, generate enthusiasm, and entertain; they like to help, participate in groups and fear losing their influence. Have difficulty in completing the tasks, quickly lose interest in what they are doing if it is not funny, usually arrive late, are forgetful and sarcastic at times.

- Supporters

Easy going, skilled with his hands, they say "yes" to everything, think always about the group, speak in the plural - they say "we believe that …"-. Looking for the comfort of others, they worry a lot, cry easily, and are hypersensitive, like romantic music and everything that reaches the heart. Do not know how to say no, then are resentful because are always the last ones. The supporters make decisions slowly, they are generous, altruistic, looking for family and social circles, are friendly, they prefer close relationships, are good listeners, avoid the conflict and apply diplomacy, seek safety, are sensitive to others ideas, are fair and reasonable.

It is important to understand that we are different. Some critics say that talking about quadrants of behavior is a very simplistic way of classifying people. Of course, there are combinations of the quadrants. It is important to avoid encasing the person in one quadrant only, understand that we have characteristics of at least 2 or 3 quadrants, and to understand one another, it is necessary to step in their shoes, to know what their priorities are and the way which they reach their goals in order to be empathetic.

Empathy is the ability to put yourself in another's place and understand their reasons of acting in a certain way, putting aside our own reasons, values, beliefs, and intentions; it is an essential skill for interpersonal relations.

Clara and Mirna are dominant. However, Clara is promoter-supporter while Mirna is controller-promoter. The ideal is to learn how to fluctuate in the different quadrants depending on the needs, in this way we understand and speak the language of all.

No group is better or more desirable than another. However, all complement each other in different ways. If you are going to work in a team is very good idea to have representatives from each group to balance.

Imagine for a moment that you're going to take a group trip. Suppose that the group consists only of promoters. No-one would have instructions about how to get to the site; they might not even have any idea of where they are going. If in the group were only supporters, they would not fit in any vehicle because it would lead to the entire family - or if not, they would not go- including the dog, the cat and the parrot. If only analysts formed the group, they would start programming the trip a few years in advance. Now think about the group being just controllers: each one would go his own way, because no one could agree.

Many problems in the relationships of couples, parents and children, brothers, friends, partners, could be avoided if we could understand the fact that we human beings have different forms of behavior. We refer to the way we act facing the circumstances. As children we make decisions to survive: some hide, others act aggressively, while some become jokers. We are not talking about personality.

Both Clara and Mirna are married to men whose predominant quadrant is analyst, and years back they did not understand why their husbands asked for a list to go to the market. The single idea of writing the list put both of the women in a bad mood. -The two are dominant-. Another awkward situation was due to the fact that neither Clara nor Mirna knew how to read maps, and the husbands did. -One is a doctor and the other engineer-. If there was no map or details of a trip, both men got upset, they had discussions and the children were in the middle of the situation. Now both women understand that their husbands need details and they provide them. In this way they have a better relationship with their partners.

It must be understood that no one is wrong or right. Say it in another way: they are both right. For the analyst the method is important, for the dominant it is irritating and incomprehensible. However, the two can reach the same result through different paths. It is as if they speak different languages. The idea is to learn how to speak the language of the partner while preserving their own. The result is magical.

Can harmony in couples, families, community, and business be achieved?

"Yeah!" When you understand that being different gives us the opportunity to learn from the other person and to enhance our skills. Instead of waiting for the others to understand us, let's start by understanding them.

There are signs in the way people do things that provide us with the information to place them on any of the quadrants of behavior, either by the manner of speaking, communication and body language, use of colors in their clothing, decor in your home and/or bedroom, among others.

A) Dominant-Formal= Controllers= Choleric

The drivers or controllers are motivated by tasks, time, problems solving, accepting challenges, making decisions fast. They question the status quo; they are frequently perceived as aggressive because they assume control and authority for fear that the other will take advantage of them. They are afraid of losing the dispute and not having results. Usually they dominate others, especially the supporters. They do not give time to consider the views of others, focus much on doing things "my way", and have difficulties getting along with others. They are task-oriented and want immediate results.

The room of a driver is usually the largest, with windows. The controller is able to do many things at the same time such as washing clothes, checking the e-mail, answering the telephone and cooking. The furniture of the house contributes to the impression of power and control, and is usually the most expensive and incredible furniture one can purchase. The house often has flowers and exotic plants, -carefully chosen to give the impression of power, but the driver never takes care of them. She/he has someone to do it for him/her. In addition, they have photos of the formal family photos showing each member in his role and the trips that have taken abroad. If they have financial possibilities, the home and the office get decorated by a specialist to create the feeling of power, and the colors are also powerful. This brings the message of "direct to business, don't waste time", go to the point, and do not beat around the bush. They identify themselves with animals of power such as the lion and the eagle. They used dominant colors such as red, black and gold. Their body posture is generally upright. The geometric figure that identifies them is the triangle, almost always pointing up.

B) Formal-Easy going= Analyst

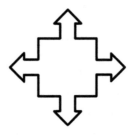

4. They get motivated by logic and details, work best if they know every aspect of the issue, use diplomacy with the people, review the precision, criticize the work, follow the authority, are often perceived as non-emotional because they are not expressive, they fear criticism and being wrong. Usually they are perfectionists. They exclude showing any feelings about decisions; they are too rigid and demanding with themselves and with others. They tend to be boring, silent and are slow to make decisions because they need all the data. They do not take many risks.

5. The room or office of an analyst is simple, does not necessarily have everything in order, but he knows where things are; he stores papers and papers – just in case. There are only articles related to what he does and he likes. It is a functional place, simple in décor; he does not like plants inside because he believes they belong to nature. Generally he uses glasses, because he reads a lot. He has diplomas hanging on the walls. He likes the colors linked to nature: coffee and dark green. The variety of music he likes is preferably from his childhood. The animal

that represents him is the owl and his geometrical figure is the rectangle or square.

C) Informals- dominants= Promoters

The promoters are very expressive and spontaneous, good motivators. They do not pay attention to details, are very global, dynamic, popular; they like getting involved with the people; they do not like to be alone. They exaggerate and generalize often, seeking harmony. They make decisions fast, are good communicators, are creative and are dreamers. They can have irrational behaviors, be egotistic, lack discipline and manipulative.

The room of a promoter is, in few words: a disaster. He loves the positive phrases and sticks them on all the walls. Things are never in place; however he/she knows exactly where each thing is and can find almost everything in any site. His colors are usually live: yellow, orange, lime green; they love sparkles in clothes; if the clothing has printing that is even better. If there are plants or flowers, they are usually dead. Either because they do not have water or are dead from the boredom of listening to the promoter talking. The promoter is a dreamer with many ideas and projects, but he does not take the time to develop any of them.

They identify with the monkey as a pet, although they have also the power of the tiger and they like to call attention to themselves like a peacock. Their geometric figure is a doodle; they spend time drawing things on paper if they are bored, and they can't sit still, they need to be in constant motion. Their body posture changes every minute, they are "scattered" when they sit down and they walk with a swing, as if they were dancing at the same time. They talk too much and like the feeling of belonging to something or someone. They are energetic and pleasant.

D) Informal-Easy going= Supporters

This type gets motivated by stability and people; they are perceived as stubborn, but they are patient. They concentrate on work, calm others, fear change. They do not complete their things as they are always helping others; they tend to yield to the wishes of others. They work well in a team, are good workers, do not take risks, do not speak for themselves.

The house or room of a supporter is characterized by having a lot of photographs of their loved ones - including pets - in all places; they use warm colors on the walls and hanging paintings of landscapes, birds and sunsets. There are flowers and plants in hallways and bathrooms. In the dressing room they use pastel colors, blue, pink, yellow and white. The furniture can be fashionable but it is not ostentatious. If you visit their home, they always have food ready and in abundance to offer and won't allow you to leave the house without taking something for your home. They enjoy cooking and taking care of the family and friends; they are saddened when left alone, and they like romantic music that reaches the heart. The geometric figure that identifies them is a circle and the animal is a lamb or a dolphin; they like physical contact and generally they like hugs and kisses.

It is important that you remember the fact that you can have a little of each quadrant, however there is one that is dominant and the others go in descending order. Understanding those differences helps us to improve relations and to establish forms of communication more effectively, both at a personal and a professional level.

In wanting to communicate with others, we do so from our own frame of reference, from what we know, that is why we have so many difficulties – translate as noise - in our relationships. Another aspect to note is that we learn in different ways.

There are three learning styles:

- Visual

  Learns from what is perceived through the eyes, is usually organized and likes to observe, worried about appearance. Tends to reflect emotions in facial gestures, has trouble remembering what he/she hears. Remembers the faces of the people, but not the names. Memorizes easily because he/she sees the words. Has a wide imagination and builds stories with mental images.

- Auditory

  Learns from listening and paying attention to all the sounds, repeats in a loud voice and moves lips; loves music and expresses emotions verbally. Usually monopolizes the conversation. Not concerned about physical appearance. Remembers names but not the faces. Not fixed on any form of drawings or illustrations, spends a lot of time singing and listening to music.

- Kinesthetic

  Learns from touching. Loves touching everything in their path, constantly moves and gesticulates a lot. Is affectionate and responds to physical signs of affection. Dresses well but does not stay like that for a long time because he/she does not remain still. Doesn't remember names or faces, but remembers the actions of people. Likes dancing and constantly changes position. Not fixed on details but on how he/she feels or the general impression that things give. Bored easily.

Check the style with which you learn and how you communicate, you do the same with the people around you, your partner, children, mom and dad, brothers and sisters, friends, partners and colleagues.

If we understand that people learn and communicate each in a different way, and therefore each has different needs than we do, we will see that our relations with all will improve for sure.

Then you can understand why your mother-in-law is as she is, says what she says, and does what she does. It is worth the effort don't you think?

Put into practice this information to become knowledgeable.

TANGLE: EVERYBODY LIMITS ME
CHANGE: I LIMIT MYSELF

TANGLE:
EVERYBODY LIMITS ME

CHANGE
I LIMIT MYSELF

AM I ABLE TO ?

From the time we are in our mother's womb, we began to receive information that is stored at the subconscious level. We don't know what is happening, but we feel.

The mother's emotions are transmitted to the baby and begin the mental programming. Then we are born and there continues a path of "training" or "domestication" to learn what apparently "is good and bad". The vocabulary is the instrument; however the vehicles of connection are the emotions. From when we are small we hear words that do not have a lot of sense but that are accompanied by specific energy - it is not what is said, but as it is said. When we are babies the phrases have tenderness, love, understanding, we start to grow and then the tone and intensity or volume change.

Imagine that a baby is starting to walk and suddenly it seems that is going to fall down. People around him yell: "Beware!" The baby does not understand the word, but experiences an emotion and frequently falls as a result of listening to the scream. With the passing of the years, he begins to hear phrases such as: "Dumb", "Stupid", and "Get out of my way", "Crybaby, Stubborn". The tones of the phrases increase as we get older.

On this basis, emotions will start to gestate and rise to a mental level. Some beliefs prevent the emotional development and become limiting ideas.

Each person has a set of ideas that are well planted in his mind. They are seeds planted by those who are closest to us, our parents, siblings, teachers, relatives, and friends. Some ideas are positive and contribute to a favorable exercise of freedom, peace and harmony; however there are many others that restrict the possibility of reaching goals and being happy.

Ideas like:

"Women are to clean, the men are to work"

"Nobody loves me because I am fat"

"Money does not by happiness"

"The rich are evil and ungrateful"

"You are dark skinned and ugly, you are never going to be more than a servant"

"The bosses are opportunists"

"You have to start from zero"

"Men do not cry"

"Life is hard"

"That's the cross you have to carry"

"A decent woman does not do that"

"Sex is bad"

"Masturbation is a sin"

"God is going to punish you"

... as well as many others.

In addition to these limiting ideas, mentally we manufacture new ones, as we combine them. This is what Aristotle called "syllogisms". The syllogism is a form of deductive reasoning where there are two premises or propositions and from them we derive a conclusion.

For example:

All men are unfaithful

My husband is a man

Conclusion: My husband is unfaithful.

Let's give men the chance to express themselves:

All women are gold diggers

My wife is a woman

Conclusion: My wife is a gold digger

In both thoughts, we must remember that the generalizations also include the idea that my dad, my brother, my uncles, my cousins, my friends, my bosses, as well as my mom, my sisters, my aunts, my cousins, fall into the same conclusion. Just think.

As these ideas have been passed from generation to generation, it would seem that they are converted into an absolute truth. The same happens with the tangles that are in other areas of your life, for example with money

The rich take advantage of the poor

My boss is rich

Conclusion: My boss takes advantage of the poor

The same happens with religion:

God punishes the sinners and sends them to hell

I am a sinner

Conclusion: God is going to punish me and send me straight to hell.

Many people don't think about whether those ideas, which they are passing on to the new generations, are something they truly believe. They simply repeat it because somebody said it.

The idea that "men don't cry", used to bolster the "machismo" image, but it causes damage at an emotional level. From childhood, boys are deprived of the possibility to express what they feel, because when they cry, both mom and dad, brothers, uncles and friends say to him: "You are a crybaby; look at the little girl", "Stop crying, faggot", "Only women cry". They think that with these ideas the child is going to feel "manly", however, the little one learns that it is a "mistake" to cry and endures pain without crying "because it is very male". With the passing of the years, he may establish a relationship in which he cannot express what he feels. So he explodes with yelling, blows and vulgarities, or takes refuge in silence, by swallowing all the pain. That suppressed emotion is then converted into physical diseases. It is well known that the number one cause of death among men is heart attacks.

Moises came to us seeking help for his family, after the death of his brother. One of the ideas tied tightly to his mind was that "problems are personal, no one has to know". These ideas had been handed down to his eldest daughter, who had been in deep silence, not venting any emotion or expressing her thoughts. Moises recalled that his father never shared what he felt, even when his son died. Neither did their brothers, they speak only of "practical and manly" things. His daughter did not cry because she learned from her father that she should not cry that she had to be strong. Thanks to his decision to improve his life, Moises and his family are now able to talk openly about what they feel and they have given themselves permission to cry and laugh more often.

This idea, by itself, might not seem to have meaning, however it depends on the perception and interpretation that each person gives to it. A girl may hear continually that "she is fat and ugly" or "she looks like a table because they have nothing in front and nothing behind". Because she stays quiet people will say that she is "shy", and they hang tags on her that she believes; and because the ideas come from the people with whom she spends most of her days, she ends up convinced that she is fat, ugly and shy and that nobody loves her. She then attracts to her life all kinds of situations where that idea is confirmed. She sabotages herself because in her subconscious mind a seed was planted long ago. She continued to cultivate the idea and believed she was not good enough. Nobody was in charge of telling her the wonderful human being she is. The fruits of those ideas are the results that she now has: low self-esteem, depression, isolation, loneliness, sadness, etc.

It is also the case that the limiting ideas surrounding money cause self-sabotage in people who grew up with premises like: "Money makes people crazy", "Money is bad and dirty", "Wash your hands you bastard! You touched money", "only poor people go to heaven". And it is not uncommon that in spite of all the effort given every day to improve their finances, and even when they add up large quantities in their bank accounts, they keep facing situations where they lose again and again. Then they say they have bad luck.

What happens is that they believe they are not worthy of having it. The idea that money causes evil, which is at the subconscious level, pops out again and again. And they themselves provoke life situations of emergency, conflict and chaos, in which they inevitably lose money.

Sergio is a hardworking, dedicated and professional man. As an immigrant he studied and obtained a license to open his business of electrical installations. In spite of his effort and the excellent quality of its service, he couldn't stay afloat or maintain a balance between his expenses and income.

While we were doing a dynamic exercise about money, Sergio recalled that as a child, his father had beaten him and his brothers quite often because one of his brothers used to get coins from his dad's trousers to buy sweets. When the father realized that, he placed the boys in a row and one by one asked them if they had taken the money. As nobody would identify the brother, all were beaten with the belt until it left marks, and sometimes bleeding wounds. The interpretation he made as a child was: "Money is bad, if you take it you get punished and you will suffer", and although it seems that the idea is absurd in an adult and, above all, a man of business, the emotions associated with the money remain the same: "I don't deserve financial success; when I get money, I get pain". Then he attracts situations in which he loses or gives away the product of his work. For Sergio, the act of charging the customer was a real torture. He ended up giving rebates to customers who did not even ask for it.

We all grew up with several or many limiting ideas; this is what our parents, teachers, brothers and friends knew and is, also, what they shared. The interesting thing is that when we became parents, we pass on these ideas to our children, unless we decide to change.

In order to begin to discard the limiting ideas, the first step is to recognize them. Make a list of the thoughts that hinder your development in the four areas: emotional, spiritual, physical and financial.

Think and write which are these ideas you grew up with and who put them in your mind.

Mirna's father told her constantly that she was "useless" because she never found the things he asked for. Often while he was fixing the car, he would scream for her to bring a tool, for example the stilton wrench. As both are strong willed, Mirna would not ask what it was or how it looked, so she would stand in front of the huge red box of tools, look and look, and then go out to the garage and say: "It is not there". She would receive the traditional scolding of: "You're useless; I don't know why I even ask you if you never find anything. You are useless!" At the subconscious level, the seed of futility had been planted long ago, from her birth, because his family had expected a boy and she arrived. She grew up with ideas such as "women are worthless", "women are products for men", which is why she attracted situations which confirmed that she was useless. It was many years later, when Mirna understood where her need to compete in order to prove that she was efficient, intelligent and useful came from. She had first to heal the relationship with her dad; then she had to forgive, release, and sow the seeds of new ideas where there was no need for competition. She had to enjoy her different roles in the development of every area of her life.

Some affirmations with which you can begin to work through the constant repetition can be:

"I am a capable person and I give my best"

"In spite of the fact that sometimes not all goes well, I am a wonderful person, intelligent and capable"

"I deserve be treated with respect and be happy"

"I love myself, I accept myself and I am an exceptional being"

One of the most moving stories happened in the course of a "tapping" or EFT (emotional freedom technique) workshop. Among those in attendance was Pepito, who then was 10 years old and was going through a complicated situation as a result of the separation of his parents. He had trouble in school and refused to do the homework and his grades began to drop considerably.

Because he was the only minor in the group, it was decided that Clara would work with the adults and Mirna would do so with the child.

They began to work on the ideas that he had of himself and when Mirna told him to repeat: "Even though I do not want to do the homework, I am a wonderful boy", the child's eyes opened wide and the smile appeared on his face. He remained silent while she repeated aloud: "In spite of the fact that I don't like go to school, I am a wonderful boy", he had an attack of laughter and said: "Am I really what you are saying?" Mirna replied: "Of course!" "The fact that you don't want to go to classes or do the homework, does not affect in the slightest the fact that you are wonderful. " Do or do you not believe that you are?" He thought about it a few seconds and said: "Yeah and I like it!" Mirna had told him that she also thought he was wonderful, but that did not have any value if he did not believe it. The next day, his mom talked to us sharing the news of that on the way back to the house, while she drove, Pepito did his homework. The following week, the child attended a seminar that we give for boys and girls, and instead of putting his name on a badge he wrote AWESOME.

In general, people are set in their results and not in the source. If they do not find a partner they complain that others are lucky and they aren't. If the business or work is going bad, they blame others and make them responsible for any financial disaster, when the truth is that they must look at what's inside and find the ideas which limit them.

In the immigrant community with which we work mostly at Avante, we find many people who are self-limiting because they do not have documents to work. They blame the government, politics, and the police, for all their misery, despite the fact that there is also another large group of immigrants which has moved forward in spite of not yet having the legal documents to live and work in the United States.

Maricela complained bitterly of the job she had. She hated to go to her office and remembered that in her country of origin she had college degrees and had begun to exercise her profession. However, she decided to move to the United States and her diploma just hung on the wall. She performed a monotonous job that she hated, arguing that she had no other option due to the lack of legal documents for work.

Months later her working papers came. But she remained in the same position for years! When she started her work in personal development, she realized that the lack of papers was only a pretext; in reality she had a fear of failure, a fear of not getting ahead, a fear of defrauding her family who had helped her. Fear paralyzed her. Understanding the origin of her fears, she started her changes. First, she quit her job - in spite of the fear of her husband, who did not have a fixed income and in spite of the country being in full economic recession - Maricela began looking for the job that was her real passion: teaching. Very soon she found what she was looking for.

Others argue that they cannot get ahead because they don't speak English, and "Without English we are nothing". When they believe this idea, their results are consistent. It is also true that there are many people who despite not speaking English have found the way to be successful either because they attend classes, study by internet or audiovisual media, request support, etc.

These people move and do everything they can to grow, learn and share. Others claim that they are discriminated against by "the gueros" because they are dark and with dark hair.

In this sense it should be noted that there is discrimination also in the countries where we originated. Clara is Colombian and in her country there is a population with African-American roots. This population has been marginalized for hundreds of years. The same is true in Mexico, where the people of the north belittle the people of the south because they are "dark skinned and ignorant". What's more, within the same families the one with white complexion is preferred over the "dark skin".

The latter get nicknames such as "Prieto", "El Chanate", "Monkey", and others.

On one occasion a lady came to the seminar with two of her daughters, both beautiful, one with dark skin and the other with pale skin. The mom told us: "This one is really beautiful because she got the family genes, we are all white, and the other one is also pretty even though she is "prietita" ("dark skinned")

Can you imagine the conclusions the girl are making on a mental and an emotional level! Unknown to herself, she is using Aristotelian thought -the syllogism-

Dark-skin people are ugly

I have dark-skin

I am ugly.

To put the limitations aside requires effort, tenacity, movement, execution, and results. And this is a big commitment. Some decide to stay as they are, although they do not like it: "evil of many, consolation of fools", - miserable but with company - because as the others, too, have the same ideas, they protect each other. They remain in the same area of "comfort", although in reality they are very uncomfortable, however, it is what they know and fear dominates them. They are paralyzed.

Take the time to review your limiting ideas and how they are affecting you. Define new ideas that will help you to build a present where you untangle the negative thoughts about yourself, and as a result, the ideas about others.

Stop living inside a mental box where you move from corner to corner. There is a box with a lot of signs that show you what you need to do to be "comfortable", such as: "he who does not trick others does not move forward", "poor but happy", "this is my cross", "if I complain they fire me ", "there is no reason to change, everybody else should change".

The comfort zone is a dangerous zone because it stalls the initiative and creation. The instructions for getting out of the box, this mental prison full of cobwebs and tangles, are outside. You have to get out in order to be able to read those instructions and act.

TANGLE: I WANT REVENGE TO DO JUSTICE
CHANGE: I WANT TO UNDERSTAND TO BE IN PEACE

TANGLE:

I WANT JUSTICE THROUGH REVENGE

CHANGE:

I WANT TO UNDERSTAND,
SO I CAN BE AT PEACE

What happens when someone does or says something that you interpret as offensive or painful? What are you doing? How do you react or respond? Do you remember any occasion in which someone did not greet you, called you dumb or ignorant, ignored your point of view, passed you on the highway and then insulted you? What changes did you feel in your body, in your emotions, in your day?

If someone does or says something that you interpret as offensive, usually you initiate a process which we call the 3 "R".

The interesting thing is that you repeat this process several times a day, each time that you remember what happened. And each time you repeat it, you are destroying yourself little by little, and therefore you affect those who are around you. It is a process so harmful that -we assure you- is the cause of the dissolution of societies, marriages, family relations, companies and the cause of wars in the world. It focuses on devastating emotions of resentment and guilt.

At the time that someone does or says something that you interpret as offensive, you start with the resentment. This often happens because the other person does not fill your expectations. In the same way you can cause these feelings in the other person when you do not fill their expectations. It is important to note that on many occasions you have no idea what those expectations are. You are full of anger, resentment, pain, fear, sadness and feel these emotions in your whole body again and again. They manifest in the form of headache or stomachache, pressure in the chest, anguish, nausea, diarrhea and many other physical conditions.

Blame someone else for your emotions, your mood and therefore your results. Since the other person is guilty, the solution is also in his hands. You expect that someone is more involved in the situation, you trust that the other person will change. Your life will also change. Little by little you learn to live in slavery. You become a victim, conduct yourself as such and live that way.

You're falling into a very destructive cycle. Each time you remember the event you feel the same emotions of rage and anger, that is why it is called RE-SENTIMENT. When the resentment is stored for a long time it can lead to diseases such as cancer, diabetes, arthritis, and others.

After the resentment comes RESISTANCE -second R-. In this part of the process you justify, question, doubt, in general you put a barrier between the other person and yourself. Possibly you stop talking to him, ignore him and strengthen the idea that you are someone's victim, they are abusing you. The process may take a couple of seconds or several hours. In many cases it can last years.

And with this sentiment is the wish that the other person "feel what you're feeling", you want to do justice. In reality what you are looking for is REVENGE -third R. You think that if you get the other person to feel what you're feeling, you will get a little relief; you will feel better. You look for a way to get even and when you finally do it, perhaps you feel a temporary relief. But then you realize that the anger and rage return and they sometimes return stronger and amplified. What is more, now you feel guilt for what you did.

You direct that anger toward yourself and live the process of the 3 R's, now directed toward yourself. You're self-punishing and destroying, in ways that are sometimes subtle and others obvious - there are those who stop eating while others eat excessively. And when you think you've calmed down, you remember the incident and again feel the anger and rage toward the other person and repeat this process which robs your peace one more time.

How many times have you felt the pain caused by a word, a beating, a rejection of your parents? Each time that you remember you suffer. When you remember your childhood, do you feel joy or sadness, tranquility or anger, hatred or love? Just as if you're living it again.

Laura felt deeply sad to recall the fact that her elder brother rejected her constantly when they were children. Every time she tried to hug him, he rejected her abruptly. Later she realized that her brother believed that their parents "preferred" her, and that is why he rejected her. However, each time that Laura remembered the incident, the sadness overtook her.

Ramiro lived in a similar situation. He said that his father rarely played with him when he was a child, because he was always traveling, and when the dad got home he was always tired. Ramiro is a father and his eyes filled with tears when he was talking about the issue. Almost thirty years has passed and the pain was still present.

Remember that the subconscious does not differentiate between fantasy and reality. When the memories of the past come to your memory, your subconscious perceives them as if they were happening in the present and the emotions are felt again.

It is therefore important that you make changes at the subconscious level. So you can release yourself from emotions that enslave you and not let you move forward. You can continue as now and keep waiting for someone to change so that your life will improve, or you can decide to take control of your life learning how to break this cycle of resentment and guilt. Choose between living with intensity or living in mediocrity.

TANGLE: I FORGIVE, BUT I DO NOT FORGET
CHANGE: TO FORGIVE IS TO UNDERSTAND

TANGLE:

I FORGIVE, BUT I DON'T FORGET

CHANGE:

TO FORGIVE IS TO UNDERSTAND

The key to breaking this cycle is forgiveness. It is important to clarify that when we speak of forgiveness we do it outside the religious context. Whatever your belief, forgiveness opens the doors to peace and happiness. Forgiveness enables you to learn to be happy in spite of …

We are going to clear some myths about forgiveness and to do this it is necessary to speak of what is not forgiveness. People say "I forgive but not forget", and we just wanted to explain that of course that you will not forget. Forgiveness does not cause partial or total amnesia. What happens is that you will remember differently. You are going to reinterpret in such a way that when you remember the event, you'll understand and you will see the learning experience. Then you will understand that you can use this experience to grow, improve and learn.

To forgive does not mean to remain in the situation.

Estela told us that her partner beat her and then asked forgiveness. She forgave and after a few days he beat her again. We explained to her that forgiveness is something different. When you forgive you understand that the person is only giving what he has and is doing what he knows; however, you don't have to accept it if it is not what you want for your life.

If you forgive you can drive away from the person in peace, without trial, without anger or resentment, and you can allow him to follow his path. There are those who are separated from their partners due to domestic violence, and do not realize that they remain enslaved because every time they remember the past they suffer again.

The physical separation is not a guarantee of emotional separation. It is important to make clear that forgiveness does not mean enduring or accepting a situation that you do not want for your life.

Forgiving is not something that is done in a minute or two. Forgiveness is a process.

In forgiving it is not necessary that the person ask for forgiveness, or to change or to repent. There is no difference if the person is alive or dead, if you live far away or close to that person.

Forgiveness is not a process for the other person; rather it is by and for you.

You're probably wondering what it is to forgive and how it is done.

Forgiveness is to understand, and release; it is to let go completely. Forgiveness is a process that allows you to be able to remember your past with gratitude and peace, it lets you make decisions and respect those of others, it lets you live in excellence, and to be happy in spite of the past.

To forgive is essential, first, that you look within yourself, review your past and the interpretations that you have made of the events that happened while growing up. You must recognize and accept emotions that you associate with each event and give yourself permission to feel them without judgment. Then you need to reinterpret what happened and find ways to learn from it. Finally, to complete the process, you must be thankful.

Ana, a participant at our seminar, was bothered with this last point, and with a bitter tone told us: "So on top of him being unfaithful to me, I have to thank him?! Nice story! We helped her to see the gift in her experience, - despite the pain of separation because she grew up with the idea that marriage is forever. Prior to the divorce, Ana changed employment to obtain a greater income. Thanks to her efficiency, -coupled with the idea of monetary need – she rose from a lesser position and salary. She also started her multi-level marketing business adventure, received training in personal development, generated residual income, met a lot of people, and socialized with ease -something that annoyed her husband - however, there was no longer screaming in the house, the children were calm because they did not hear fights and they were not afraid as they used to be when their parents stopped talking to each other for long periods of time.

Calm returned to the home. Ana opened a universe of possibilities; she began to do things that before she dared not, she became independent financially and emotionally. Don't you think it would be good to thank your husband? We went back to ask her. She nodded laughing loudly.

We compared the process of forgiveness with the cleaning of the closet. First you need to open the door, see what is in there, inspect to decide what serves you and what doesn't; remove what you don't need or don't want to and then reorganize what is left and leave enough space to put new things. However, if there is empty space, this will fill up quickly and soon you will have your closet messy again; unless you consciously put there only what you want.

As it happens with the cleanliness of the closet, it is not easy to get started. Do you remember how you feel when you are about to clean it? You feel lazy, sigh and leave it for another day. You know that it is full of things in disarray, some really unnecessary and others which are just garbage, but you keep it "just in case". Although you are aware of the need to clean it you procrastinate. Then you look to your partner, your children, your brothers, your work colleague's closet and criticize them for their mess. It is easier, isn't it?

You get busy with other activities that you use as an excuse for not cleaning your mental closet, which is full of ideas, values, emotions, beliefs and experiences. Some of them help you grow and others destroy you. Sometimes it's scary to open that mental closet, and you pretend that all is well and that it is organized as you want. At the end of the day you say you are not organized anyway. In fact, you do not even know what's in there .

Remember that when we refer to the mental closet we are talking about your subconscious, your automatic pilot, the genie of the lamp, the magic wand.

If it is crammed full of things and you open the door, everything falls over. If it is filled over its capacity the door usually does not resist and opens by itself. When you are under a stress your closet opens and what is inside comes out. You can keep the door closed at times while you are aware. However, as most of the time you are running on auto-pilot, the door opens mechanically and all those saved emotions come out when you receive some external stimulus like the weather, financial situation, your partner says or does something, your children, your friends, your boss and countless other situations and people.

You get upset and assert that what came out is because of someone else, or that it came out of the closet of your neighbor. Remember that the guardian of the closet, your conscious, is asleep most of the time and your wardrobe is filled with things without you knowing it. And there are certainly a few dead rats in there. The dead rats represent those emotions such as hatred, sadness, loneliness, guilt, anger, and all the variants of emotions that are classified as negative. It is difficult for some to accept that they have them, because dead rats make them feel guilty. In the process of forgiveness, recognize that they are part of the range of emotions with which you live and are not only important but essential.

Emotions are not good or bad, positive or negative, they just are. To feel is healthy. To judge is hurtful.

Now your mental closet is open and you get the opportunity to look and recognize what is inside. The next step is to review and decide which of these emotions, values or ideas you want to keep and which ones you want to get rid of.

And it comes time to discard what you do not want. So you free up space to fill it with what you want. In cleaning you feel lighter, relaxed, calm, at peace, free. To complete the process you need to put in only what you want.

This is your chance to decide what you want to fit into the place that was empty. Now you can begin designing your own life, your destiny, your present and your future. And if you want to be free, then this is the time to fit in peace, love, understanding, tolerance, understanding, compassion and your process of forgiveness is complete.

It is important to repeat this process several times in order to heal fully. Just like when you have a wound; you need to change the dressings on several occasions until the wound closes completely and heals. Forgiveness must be converted into a daily habit if you want to remain at peace, because situations happen daily and many times you interpret them as offensive, you need to re-interpret them to avoid resentment and guilt.

Frank grew up in a household with an alcoholic dad who often brutally beat and insulted his mother. He recalled all the anger and helplessness he felt each time his father came home drunk to beat them. Frank dreamed of the day in which he could remove his mother from that situation. He wanted with all his heart be big enough to defend his mother. He ran away from home as a young boy and began to work. He saved with much love and with great courage the memory of his mother and held on to his hatred of his father. He believed that his mother had been a saint to withstand so much abuse.

One day he returned to the house and offered to pay for an apartment for his mom so that she could liberate herself from the beatings and insults. His mother did not accept the offer. She explained to Frank that she loved her husband —according to her, he was changing over the years. Frank felt much pain and confusion, had sworn he would never do the same thing as his father. He left home again. Then he got married.

He came to AVANTE looking for help because he was destroying his relationship by yelling and beating up his children. He was living full of rage and anger. During the self-development work he had the opportunity to open his mental closet and watch all those emotions that there had been accumulating over the years. We suggested that he open himself to the possibility that his anger was not only against his father but also against his mother. His immediate response was "It would be unfair to feel anger towards my mother, she sacrificed herself for us, the poor woman suffered very much, how can I feel something that is not love toward her?"

However, as the inner work continued he realized and accepted the idea that actually he felt anger toward his mother for having accepted the situation, for not having had the courage to be separated and in this way have avoided the damage.

As he began to accept his true feelings, he also began to re-interpret his past and to understand that his parents had done what they knew.

He enquired about the life stories of his parents and discovered all the pain, fear and anger that his parents had inherited from their own parents. With this information it was easier to work on his own re-interpretation and to find the value in his experiences. For example, he recognized that due to the violence of his home and his dream of helping his mother, he had the strength to work hard, save, stay away from drugs and alcohol, and move forward. He began to thank his parents for what they gave him, because he understood that that was all that they had. He also understood that he could be different and break the chains of violence.

Your actions are determined by your emotions; if you allow others to control your emotions, then who really directs your life? "I do not like anyone telling me what to do" people say while they allow resentment and guilt to lead their lives. And what is most interesting is that in many cases these people that apparently did us harm, are not aware of that. Some live on the other side of the world or perhaps have already died.

Why do we say that they direct your life? Think about it. Each time that you remember any past event you feel again the anger, pain, or fear and act in accordance with that emotion. However, if you forgive, if you let go, and if you become responsible when you remember, you choose how you want to feel and act.

Frequently people arrive at the seminars who have had the experience of sexual abuse at different ages and usually by relatives or people nearby.

The most common question is how am I supposed to forgive someone who did me so much harm? In most cases the event occurred during childhood and since then, the person has brought with him/her the anger, the feeling of helplessness, shame, guilt and other emotions that are still hurting and which will continue to do so.

The options we offer them are:

1. To live miserably and to continue with the cycle of negative emotions

2. To forgive and free themselves to live in excellence

Re-interpreting the sexual abuse is not easy. Some of the factors that come into play are the fact that, at times, the child liked the touch and he went so far as to believe that that is the way to play or connect with others. When he grows up and becomes aware of what happened, he feels ashamed and guilty. The process of forgiveness must include not only the victimizer, who on many occasions was a victim himself at some point of his life, but also to the victims, who supposedly could have avoided the abuse, as parents, grandparents and family members.

One of Clara's experiences was sexual abuse as a child. She recalls that some of the interpretations she made for many years about her experience of abuse were:

- My parents do not love me, since they did not protect me

- I did something wrong, my parents are good people, and if they did not protect me it was because I did not deserve it, which it means I am a bad person.

- I must be a very bad person since I like it.

- I am ashamed because I did not say anything.

- I am a coward because I did not have the courage to say something and avoid the abuse

All of these interpretations filled her with anger, shame, pain, fear, doubt and hatred. Until her teens she was a silent and submissive girl. Then, during her adolescence, the rage and outrage toward her family was so much, that she "became" a rebel.

She decided to "forget" what had happened without talking it over with anyone else. She internalized all the emotions and memories of the past. She thought that this was the solution and continued her life pretending that everything was fine. She closed the door of the closet with force.

All went reasonably well for some time. Then she moved to the United States following the dream to maintain her marriage, and with the pressure of the cultural shock the closet door began to open. These emotions saved for so many years poured out with increasing frequency and her life became a living hell inside. She could not remember the events of the past and did not understand what was going on in her life. Professionally she continued to have much success and the more success she had, the worse she got emotionally.

Finally the answers to her questions appeared. In spite of fear, she attended a three day personal development seminar. There she was given the opportunity to look inside. She learned the power of forgiveness and the re-interpretation. From that day on she started to enjoy life. This happened more than 20 years ago.

Some of the new interpretations Clara made were:

- My parents protected me the only way they knew. They were not prepared to foresee this type of situation because nobody taught them.

- My parents love me very much and the abuse had nothing to do with the love they have for me.

- I am a good person and I did what a child my age would do, considering the experience and information I had at that age.

- The victimizer was possibly a victim at some point, and then did what he knew. His conduct has no relationship with my value as a human being.

- Thanks to that experience I learned to be sensitive, to forgive, to understand and - without noticing it - I was being prepared to fulfill my mission in life, to share the message of the power of forgiveness.

- Thanks to that experience I know the difference between living in an inferno of hatred, shame, and courage, and live in the sky that provides the peace that forgiveness provide.

You can't change the facts, but you can change the interpretation. It is a decision between being a slave or living as a free person, being a victim or being responsible, living or just vegetating.

For a long time Clara sabotaged each success she was having, because, basically she did not believe that she deserved it. She thought she had done something wrong and therefore was still self-punishing. Forgiveness allowed her to be free.

On one occasion, when interviewing a rape victim, the woman commented that she had forgiven her attacker. The journalist asked, with an expression of disbelief that he could not avoid, how was it possible to forgive someone who had done so much damage? Her answer was simple and direct: "He destroyed one day of my life, I am not going to allow him to damage one more". That is a good reason to forgive.

If you want to give permission to others to build or destroy your life instead of doing it yourself, it is simple. The only thing you have to do is to keep the resentment or to forgive. The decision is yours.

In many occasions we need help to forgive. Look for help. Find the way. The path shortens and gets easier when we walk it holding hands with someone else.

Forgiveness should be a daily habit. This takes you to the path of no judgment, looking for ways to understand and re-interpret each situation in your life. Little by Little you become a "good" finder. You understand each person has his own story, and you will never have all the facts to make a fair judgment.

If you want to be happy in spite of circumstances, forgive, understand, let go and practice compassion.

The truth is that freedom lies on being able to choose how you want to feel in each circumstance, in the face of any situation.

TANGLE: I AM A VICTIM
CHANGE: I AM RESPONSIBLE

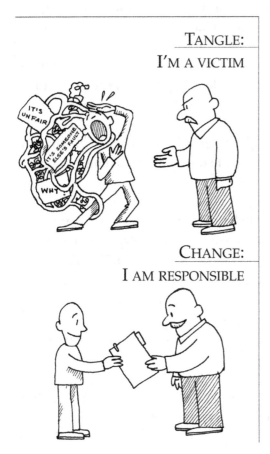

TANGLE:

I'M A VICTIM

CHANGE:

I AM RESPONSIBLE

There is a disease that is destroying the world. It is an epidemic that is taking alarming dimensions. The name of this disease is VICTIMITIS. Those who suffer it throw phrases such as:

- It's your fault that I am sad

- You make me mad!

- Do you see this grey hair? It's your fault!

- I can't live without you, I will die!

- I get upset because of you!

- If you had not done this, I would not feel the way I do!

- Why does this happen to me?

- God did not want that for me!

- God will punish him

- Because of my parents I am the way I am!

- Life is unfair!

- Poor me!

- Nobody understands me, everybody mistreats me!

We could continue writing innumerable phrases like those, because the ones who suffer from "victimitis" have a complete dictionary: VICTIM MANUAL updated and revised.

Be very careful, this disease is highly contagious. It transmits from parents to children, among siblings, friends, from teachers to students and vice versa, bosses to employees, employees to bosses, amid strangers; from direct contact or long distance, sometimes slowly and other pretty fast; it does not discriminate among color, language, age, sex.

It makes you a slave, kills you little by little, destroys you and everything around you, it does not allow you to move or it makes you move very slowly, it guides you to paths of sadness, rage, anger, deception, resentment, and loneliness.

The Victimitis is learned at a very early age at home. Remember if your parents used to complain about how ungrateful you were, since you did not notice how hard they worked to give you everything. Those times when they beat you up and yelled at you affirming it was your fault. That day you broke the cup and they screamed at you for being careless. Remember the fear you had to admit you made a mistake because you knew you were going to be punished, and then you saved yourself by using the technique of blaming others?

Pablito's face was muddied with chocolate when his mom intentionally asked: "Who ate the chocolate cake without my permission?" The child was shaken while his mouth was still full and he raised his hand to point to his little brother less than a year of age. The story is real, and is repeated too often in families

What did you feel when you heard your parents blaming the government, the boss, the mother, the neighbor or anyone else, for the situation in which they were living?

Blaming, accusing, and pointing fingers are the daily bread in many houses. It is easier to blame others than to take responsibility. However the price paid for not assuming responsibility is quite large.

You can avoid your responsibility, but you can't avoid the consequences that follow. When you don't take responsibility and blame others, you are giving up control of your life to those you blame. If the others are guilty of your mood or your results, then you need wait until they change or modify their way of being or to act for your life to change. It is certainly convenient, but the price is high. You are paying with your life. You stop learning, growing, and living.

And when you become responsible for another, you limit and obstruct them. The result is resentment on the part of the other person. You think you're doing them a favor and in reality you're destroying them little by little. If you are responsible for the happiness of the other, then also you're responsible for their misery. It is a very heavy burden to carry.

There are ways to diagnose the disease and one of them is the vocabulary that is used. The ones suffering from victimitis very often used words such as:

-   I could, I should, I would, it is difficult, impossible, I have to, I can't, it is your fault. People who suffer from victimitis talk with each other every detail of "what was done to them" - they never mention what they did

-   Their talks are always in past time, they cry often, they get angry if others do not pay attention to them, and they get very upset if you tell them they are suffering from "acute victimitis"

- They are offended because they have not been able to see themselves. They believe they are fine; the others are wrong and do things wrong without any consideration.

- They won't talk with you for months or years, convinced that you offended them, simply because they didn't like what they heard.

The marvelous thing is that there is an effective antidote to cure the acute victimitis. It is called: RESPONSIBILITY

Begin to take responsibility for your life. Grab the reins of your present. Decide for yourself. Stop blaming, pointing fingers, and judging. Focus on solutions, learning and growing.

You must be asking, how do I do that? Here we offer you some steps:

1. First, accept that there is a problem. It is impossible to solve a problem if you do not accept that there is one. Pay attention to your vocabulary. Review your attitudes, do you judge, point fingers, blame, accuse?

2. After you diagnose the problem, decide what you are going to do about it. If you decide to take control over your life, start by changing your vocabulary and learn to re-interpret life situations.

Instead of:	Say:
"You make me mad"	"I got mad"
"You make me happy"	"I decide to be happy"
"It is your fault I feel sad"	"I am sad"
"Nobody understands me"	"I want to understand"

3. Be thankful. When you see an opportunity for learning and growing in each situation, your need to blame and judge must

disappear. Instead, show gratitude. Being thankful is one of the best tools to stop pointing fingers and judging. As you focus on what you have, on the positive, the good, abundance, you move forward in the process of regaining the control of your destiny.

The people or circumstances that you attract to your life are tools for mutual personal growth. Unfortunately a large number of people do not recognize it, and waste the opportunity to become student-teacher. You learn and teach simultaneously on a daily basis, consciously or subconsciously.

Next time you feel someone did something to you, remember "you attract him or her to your life and ask: "What do I need to learn from this situation or this person? Where is the learning? Instead of asking, "why me", ask "why to me?"

Ricardo complained that his six year old daughter "made him mad, desperate". He blamed her for his lack of control which usually ended up in screams. We suggested he thank his daughter and look at her as "his teacher". "My teacher?" he responded in surprise. We explained that those we consider a nuisance and become a headache are precisely our best teachers. They give you the opportunity to practice patience, love and compassion. They facilitate your looking inside yourself.

With time the father-daughter relationship has improved, and as Ricardo works on his personal growth he has learned to control his emotions, instead of being a puppet for his daughter.

The only thing that can come out is what's inside. Dr. Wayne Dyer, considered one of the "greatest spiritual leaders" and author of more than 30 books, explained using a beautiful analogy:

"When we squeeze an orange, we get orange juice, because that is what an orange has inside. The same is true with us. When we get squeezed what's inside of us comes out". How do we get squeezed? By our children, partner, siblings, and in general anyone who is close to us. We get squeezed by the weather, the government, the news and all the circumstances we consider negative. Usually our first reaction is an animalistic one. There is no space between the stimulus and the reaction. This is the way many individuals operate. "The heat makes me mad and the cold depresses me" people comment. You blame the stimulus for your response, which means you have no conscious control over your response.

It is essential to understand that only what's inside of you comes out and if you do not like it you can change it. If what comes out is anger, hate, resentment, sadness, that's what you have inside. If there is peace, love, comprehension, compassion, tolerance, that will come out because that's what's inside.

It is impossible for peace to come out if you are full of rage. It is like pretending that when your closet is full of garbage, you open the door that flowers will pour out.

Enrique established a partnership and few weeks later problems started because he realized his partners were trying to open their own independent businesses. He got very upset —according to him- he had opened his heart and helped them and they betrayed him by taking away customers and keeping the group's money. He reacted with anger; he screamed, cursed and swore and wanted to go to beat them. He felt victimized and spent the time telling everyone who would listen what had happened.

He did not realize that real responsibility would be to allow the person to respond, it was not responsible to react.

He had decided to open the partnership, the results were his responsibility. This "problematic" situation gave Enrique the opportunity to find new and better partners, find new mechanisms and expand his business to different areas. In reality, the problem was a gift in disguise. It took some time for him to assimilate this new idea; however, he began changing his way of thinking and his aggressiveness, and started to walk the path of understanding.

When the stimulus is received, it is a good idea to take some time so you can respond consciously. As what's inside is changing, your responses change too and reflect the inside. Your results are just a reflection of your interior. Change your inner state and your results change too. It is a decision. It is the real freedom.

In the process of accepting responsibility, it is important to understand that each person does what he can with what he has. You can't give what you don't have. Every human being has his own story and therefore also has his own tangles with which to filter the information he receives. And you're not different than anyone else.

Remember: become a seeker of the good. Take advantage of every opportunity to learn, to grow. Look for the positive in every situation and appreciate it.

If you want to live in fullness it is essential that you heal the "acute victimitis" because not only does it affect you, but it is contagious.

TANGLE: FACTS ARE IMPORTANT
CHANGE: WHAT IS IMPORTANT IS THE INTERPRETATION

TANGLE:

FACTS ARE IMPORTANT

CHANGE:

INTERPRETATION IS MOST IMPORTANT

Upon the occurrence of a situation where the emotions are altered, individuals make their interpretations from the perception of the facts. That is why in a home where there are four or five children, although they are physically similar, they may give the impression of having been raised by different parents. Emotionally they are different, and they interpret each fact in different ways

Let's say that there are several children in the family and in that house there has been domestic violence, both verbal and physical abuse. The fact is the same; however, each child perceives it differently and makes decisions on the basis of this interpretation.

If one or several of the children have fretful temperaments, i.e. dominant and drivers, they may wish to confront the perpetrator. If they do not, they may hold resentment because of what they saw and have ideas such as: "I will never allow someone to do that to me, when I grow up I will get even", "Why does she permit that, why does she tolerate it?" "My father is a miserable human being, then all men are miserable human beings".

Another kid with melancholic temperament and supporter behavior may get scared and may think: "Maybe I did something wrong and it is my fault, I need to find a way to solve this situation".

Based on the same situation, different decisions are made. Parents yell and insult each other, but each child perceives it differently. The aggressive girl is not going to allow men to abuse her; the passive one —because she is afraid- is going to be looking for ways to win affection and solve the problem which she thinks she cause. Reality is one thing, interpretation is another.

Then, what's more important, the facts or the interpretation? Can we change the past? No. Do we have the ability to change the interpretation? Of course! We can interpret however we want.

Maria lived in a domestic violence situation. Her father was a very aggressive man —he grew up in an environment of physical and verbal abuse. This is what he learned and gave. The real fact is that the father beat and insulted her, made pitiful comparisons and used many vulgarities. As a child she made interpretations that caused pain and hurt, and that put her today in an abusive relationship of her own. As an adult she can change her interpretations. She can say her dad was miserable, a beast, or can understand and say her dad was a guy who lived and grew up with a lot of pain, resentment and lack of love, that all he knew was to yell and insult. The situation has nothing to do with her. She can begin to plant a new idea in her mind, to heal the emotional wounds of the past: "I am a worthy person, I deserve the best, and my dad just did what he did because that was all he knew".

Which of the two interpretations would help María to find peace and calm? Will any of the interpretations change the past? No. The fact remains: the same beatings, same insults, and same humiliation. That won't change; however according to the interpretation, the present could change, and by changing the present your results follow.

The fact does not change, the interpretation makes the difference between being a happy person or a miserable one. The value is there. The fact is a fact, what happens stands, it does not matter what your interpretation might be. Remember the example we gave before: you are driving and someone passes you almost causing an accident. The fact is: someone just passes you. The interpretation could be: "This stupid does not know how to drive" or "Maybe he is sick, has someone at the hospital or is in a big hurry". Does the real situation change? No, it does not change. Your attitude can change, your thinking can change, your feelings can change and your results too can change. What would happen if I got upset and said: "This is stupid". Some people accelerate, move forward and get in front of the other "to see what it feels like", or get tachycardia, insulting the other driver during all the way and arrive at the office or at the house with all that outrage. When the child greets him happily, what the child will get in response is "Get out of here, I am in a bad mood because a stupid —most likely he will use some other heavy language- went past me!

The interpretation of the facts determines your results: you either are happy or angry and resentful, making life miserable for everybody.

Reinterpret the past - when there is resentment-, it is of the utmost importance to undo the tangles that are there in the mind, heart and soul of the people. You may believe that you are fooling yourself because the reality was different, however you've created that reality and have the possibility of reinterpreting it and forgiving.

Being given the opportunity to change the interpretation through forgiveness and understanding means having the opportunity to live with intensity, without chains and shackles to a painful past that, if not healed, will be inherited by those who are closest to us.

Clara shared with you her experience of sexual abuse. The fact will not change, the experience was there. By changing her interpretation, her whole life has changed.

There are those who cry out to the four winds: "justice must be done". For the sake of justice, we get hurt and hurt the whole world, because what in reality is being sought is revenge. We don't want to say to ignore the abuse of any kind; what we want to say is that the murderer, the victimizer, the person who is abusing another, has his own history of pain, suffering, resentment and anger. In the cases of physical, sexual and emotional abuse, most likely it is that the victimizer has also been a victim in his early years and therefore only repeats what he learned. He also needs help. In some cases the only way to help them is to put them away from society.

By being able to see the victimizers with eyes of understanding, rather than lifting the accusing finger, we gain the opportunity to send positive energy to the Universe. If you have lived through an abusive situation, in any of its forms, it is important that you ask yourself: Why am I going to let that fact keep hurting me? Am I going to continue carrying this guilt, resentment and anger? Who is most affected by those painful interpretations of my past? How long am I going to let that person or persons controlling my emotions and affect my present?

Being happy is a decision. Remember you can't change your past, you can change however the way you interpret it.

TANGLE: LIFE IS A GAME OF RUSSIAN ROULETTE
CHANGE: LIFE IS A WHEEL

TANGLE:
LIFE IS PLAYING RUSSIAN ROULETTE

CHANGE:
LIFE IS A WHEEL

We live with the foot on the accelerator, we eat fast, we hardly sleep and we laugh shortly. There is more media and we communicate less. We have more TVs, telephones and computers at home than books. We no longer speak, we only "send text messages"; we spend a lot of time on Facebook reviewing the messages from people we don't even know instead of socializing. Time passes quickly, and often we are exhausted. We pay attention to what we consider to be a priority and we put aside what is important.

Our life is composed of different areas that are linked to achieve balance and well-being. However, it is very common that greater attention is given to one or two, while neglecting the rest. There are those who focus on work, and set aside recreation and even rest; others build their bodies with exercise and food, and neglect the emotional side; some people think that what is most important is to have things: a car, a home, money, and they forget the spiritual connection.

Various authors mention that there are seven areas of human development ; others say that there are ten. For the purpose of the work that we do through the seminars, we will use four major areas, although there are subdivisions.

- Emotional

- Spiritual

- Physical

- Financial

How can we know if we are in balance or out of it? Be totally honest when performing the following exercise. It is important to think about the fact in order to know where you want to go, first you need to know where you are right now. Just like when you're going to make an air reservation, the first thing they ask you is: "What is the city of origin?" and "Then where are you going?".

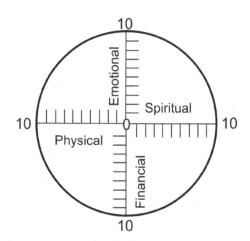

In the circle are the four areas of development, and there are small notches from the center toward the periphery. In the center is the 0 which is equivalent to nothing and the 10 is the maximum score.

Find a comfortable position that allows you to be relaxed and without interruptions allowing you to clear your mind.

The emotional part includes –among other things- personal development, education, profession, performance satisfaction, family and social relationships, communication abilities, socialization, recreation, friendship and loving relationships. To evaluate this area start by thinking about your relationship with your parents, siblings, children, partner, in-laws, etc. Are you satisfied with the way you handle your family relationships? Do you have good communication, or do you prefer not to count on them? Are there misunderstandings, resentments, anger, rage accumulated through the years? Are you happy with those relationships? On the other hand, how are your friendships? Do you have few or many friends? Do you socialize or do you have a hard time with that? Do you prefer to isolate yourself or are you the "heart of the party"? Do you consider yourself introverted or extroverted? Are you satisfied with the way you relate to others? Think about how you relate with your community, neighbors, employees or employers, co-workers. Ask yourself if you feel professionally satisfied: are you at the professional level you want to be? Have you accomplished all your goals and are you setting new ones? Do you pursue your dreams or you wait for things to change so you can make your move? Are you performing the activity that you really love or you're bored with what you do? Are you satisfied with your results? What level of 0 to 10 you think you are? Put a mark on the number that you think, according to where you feel you are at this time. It is not a question of projecting, but to be congruent with your present results.

Now, go to the spiritual area. Reflect on your inner peace and the purpose of your life. Spirituality is not the same as religion, you can be religious and not be spiritual, or be spiritual without having any religion. It is the connection with your source, with your Higher-Self, the sensation of belonging to a bigger source. You can call it God, Superior Energy, Universe, Mahomet, Buddha, Jehovah, or any other name. The importance thing is to have a connection, beyond matter, through faith so you can believe the unbelievable and see the invisible. As the spirit finds shelter in our being, life becomes full of harmony, peace, patience, humility, kindness and joy through forgiveness.

Reflect on this area of your life. Do you feel there is a connection? Do you think that the level of commitment that you have so far is satisfactory, or that you can do more, because in reality you've neglected this area? Do you help your congregation, or church group? Do you help others through community service, expecting absolutely nothing in return? Can you feel inner peace and transmit it to other people? Put a mark on the number where you think you are at this stage of your life.

Now, let's move onto the physical area that includes caring and strengthening the body, the only packaging what we have and what we often neglect, because there are those who focus on the external part, that is only the appearance, forgetting that everything that is projected toward the outside, comes from inside. Think about it, when was the last time that you detoxified your body, went to a preventive medical review, measured your blood pressure and had blood tests done? Do you eat in a healthy way or you are one of those persons who tend not to feed your body, but to fill it up, eat without schedule and fast, don't drink enough pure water, have a sedentary life, are constantly stressed and don't find time for sports and relaxation, and have chronic diseases that affect your daily performance.

Answer these and other questions honestly. Put a mark on the site that you consider is the one that represents what you are doing now to keep your body in balance.

Review now the financial area. It is not just that you take a look at your portfolio, but you do a tour of everything that is included in this line, for example if you are in the economic position that you want to be, if you live successfully with the income you have. Ask yourself if you have enough money saved, or if you don't have any savings, if you are undisciplined in this line, if you save but don't know what for. Do you know how to use your credit cards or are you up to the top and you can't make the minimum payment; do you have a special fund to cover expenses for at least six months or you live day to day? Can you go on vacation freely without worrying that when you come back your debts have accumulated? If you have children, do you have life insurance and an education fund? Do you have more debts than friends? Do you have assets? Do you know how and where to invest, or are you borrowing money at all time ? Do you pay your debts or do you stay without friends because of being a "bad debtor"? Do you hate the work that you have but you tolerate it because you have outstanding payments? Can you manage unexpected expenses due to illness or death? Do you feel full and satisfied with the financial results that you have at this time? Place a mark in the number that you think you are right now.

When you have completed the assessment in the four areas, joins the marks or points by drawing a curved line following the line of the circumference.

Pay attention how it looks now and think the following:

This exercise is called "The Wheel of life". How does your wheel look? For a wheel to move forward it has to be round, all of its areas must be harmonic and balanced. Is yours like that? Or does it seem like a flying saucer, sausage, football? This gives you a clearer idea of what areas you need to work on.

Maybe you got a small wheel, well rounded but little. It means you are going to have to give more laps to move forward. If the wheel of life has not reached 10, means you need to work every day. It could be you move forward in an area and backwards in another. The important thing is that you remember the four areas and keep working to be in balance. If you are aware of your progress or lack of it, you can focus easily. If there is a lack on the spiritual areas, what are you going to do about it? Which decisions are you going to make, which measures are you

TANGLE: I HAVE DESIRES
CHANGE: I SET GOALS

TANGLE:

I HAVE DESIRES

CHANGE:

I SET GOALS

In the story of "Alice in Wonderland", the protagonist arrives at a site where there are a number of signs which indicate different routes to take. Then the Cheshire Cat appears and the conversation between the two is, more or less, as follows:

- Could you show me where to go from here?- asks Alicia.

- That depends on where you want to go- responds the cat.

- I do not care where.

- In that case, it does not matter where you go – says the feline.

When your ideas do not have a definite direction, surely you are going to be spinning in the same spot and feeling tired all the time because you don't arrive anywhere.

Hence the importance of setting goals in life, that goes beyond the idea of having just a dream. And that isn't to say that you need to stop dreaming, on the contrary, but the best way of landing those dreams is by determining the goals.

When you define the goals we need a detailed plan of action, it is not sufficient to just write them down, that is nothing more than the first step, it is necessary to focus and work on them to achieve these goals, taking into account the following features:

GOALS:

- Measurable

   To be able to measure goals gives us the opportunity to know when we reach them and how to assess them as we go.

- Specific

   The objective is to define exactly and in detail what we want.

- Time bound

   It is important to determine the starting and ending time, datelines. This facilitates being able to stay on track and make the necessary adjustments on the way.

- Attainable

   The goals need to be ambitious but within the general life plan so it is more feasible to attain them.

- Risky

   The goals need to have passion, enthusiasm and a dose of nervousness to make you get out of the comfort zone.

The goals are clear if you decide what you want to achieve and by when. If you want a new car, describe the details, the year, the brand, color, accessories, etc. If you want money, don't say, "I want to make more", because "more" is a dime or an extra dollar. Be specific with the details, for example, "I'm going to save $1, 000.00 (or pesos, yen, euros, etc.) in 30 days", and clarify the purpose of savings. If what you want is time with your family and only say: "I'm going to spend more time with my children", it is not a specific goal. You would say "I'm going to talk 20 minutes with each of my three sons, from Monday to Friday and one hour on weekends for the next three months".

It is important to remember that the mind works with images and the word NO lacks an image, so say what you want, not what you do not want. If your goal is losing weight, eliminate "I don't want to be fat" because what your mind see is an overweight person, and if the mind sees it, it will make it reality. For your goal to be powerful: "On July 31, 2012 I weigh 145 pounds".

If you already know what you want and how you're going to achieve it, you do not have a goal you have a plan. The target must pull you out of that comfort zone where you are, it should stretch you out.

People who have attended the seminar, CHALLENGE OF CHANGING YOUR LIFE, and want to continue working on themselves, enrolled in the leadership program. In that program we work with their personal goals. Each person has a mentor who helps them to focus on those goals, because there is a trend to set goals aside using innumerable excuses. Frequently people affirm that there are more important things in their lives. If you have a mentor, the way lightens, and you can achieve the goals with greater effectiveness.

Once you have defined your goals, keep it clear that it is important to develop your character as a person, learn new skills, discard old bad habits, embrace new ideas and undertake new challenges; become someone who can attract positive things and emotions in your life and be willing to work, to make mistakes, to learn. Build your identity without strapping it to the material; attach it to the greatness that you possess as a human being. Always BE, and then DO, so you can HAVE.

The majority of people have reversed the order: first make things in order to be able to have - a car, a house, a profession, etc. - and only then they can BE happy.

Focus on BE, the rest will follow.

TANGLE: I SWEAR NEVER AGAIN
CHANGE: I AM WITHOUT INTEGRITY

TANGLE:
NEVER AGAIN I SWEAR

CHANGE:
I'M OUT OF INTEGRITY

It happens frequently that when you want to make substantial changes from the inside, you take the task of setting goals and looking for mechanisms to implement them through commitments. A commitment is a unique way to face challenges, it is a required value to fulfill the mission that plays in any role of the life, whether in the family, company, school, a religious congregation, etc. The commitment benefits first of all the person who acquires it and, as a consequence everyone around.

When there is a commitment the objectives cannot be changed arbitrarily, on the contrary, they are continually revised to make sure everything is on track.

The substantial changes occur when people actually commit and give value to their words. When there is a genuine commitment, the tenacity and constant effort add to it. A committed person, always strives to go much beyond what is expected, he does not stay in a routine : he transcends what is expected and is not just part of the crowd.

The commitment is what transforms a promise into a reality. Your word ensures commitment to your intentions. For years, a verbal commitment was enough to make a business agreement. It is an agreement where the honor and integrity have a privileged position.

To seal the agreements - which are not in writing – frequently it is used phrases such as: "I promise you that I am going to do what I say". "I swear by God". "I undertake to fulfill, and if not, may lightning hit me". "Until death do us part".

Do you know these phrases? Someone has said them to you, or perhaps you used them on occasion.

However human beings are fallible, that is, we make mistakes, and sometimes -despite the commitment - we do not keep the word, we screw up, blow it, mess it up and other terms that we prefer not to mention in this space. If the commitment or the word has a value that cannot be measured in gold coins, nor in centimeters, nor inches, then how do we measure it? What is lost when it is not met?

It is interesting that some people tend to flee when not upholding their word. They disappear from the map, as if this act will erase the result of their actions. It happens more often in cases where there is money involved. They screw up and flee - with the money, of course-, leaving a trail of confusion and bitter feelings. They do not realize that their actions do not only create a precedent, but that their actions come from a history of dishonesty that is recurrent in their lives. The reality is that they have never truly committed, they spend their lives thinking they are making fool of others, when in reality the only ones who betray is themselves.

Some come forward, repent and apologize for their actions. They say things like: "I swear by God I will never do it again", "I swear this is the last time", "I swear by my mother that I do it no more". However, it is feasible that they commit the same offense in a short period of time, because the deception and lies are part of the tangles with which they have grown up.

Ricardo is a prankster. He brings out the humorous side of any incident and in one of the seminars he commented that as a child he spent time inventing fantastic stories to justify his mischievousness. Since his parents usually beat him up and shouted horrible things at him, he learned to tell lies to justify himself. His justifications were so absurd that there came a moment that instead of scolding, his parents were laughing at him. He found the mechanism to save himself from the beatings: Even when he was tagged with a mouth full of chocolate, he assured that a Martian had been eating the cake! It happens that as an adult he continued with the same pattern of wonderful stories to justify his irresponsible behavior. However, he was on the verge of divorce due to inventing stories that his wife did not appreciate.

We make mistakes, and for each error there is the possibility of rectifying the wrong. The damage cannot be eliminated, but it is possible to revive integrity, to live in accordance with an elevated state of awareness.

Being someone with integrity does not imply being perfect, and it is not a concept of morality. Like intelligence, it can be used to cause damage. A smart person is not necessarily good or happy. Integrity is an attitude that is incorporated into the daily life to obtain satisfaction, because basically it comes down to doing what is said and promised; this applies both to individuals and to organizations.

Say you have a commitment to see a business person at a given date and time, or to pick up your son from school. If you somehow miss the commitment, or you are late, your business associate may not trust your reliability or your son might be left waiting for hours. There is a cost, either monetary or a loss of image and confidence.

Something as simple as: "I have lost my integrity, what can I do to regain my integrity?" is a good beginning. The answer does not necessarily come from the other person, but from your inner being which looks for ways to find different mechanisms to comply with the agreements.

Being a person with integrity does not mean being perfect, human perfection does not exist, however we are improvable beings, our integrity speaks more loudly than words in forging our character despite the adversities.

If you are without integrity, it is a good time to re-commit and give value to your word.

TANGLE: I DO NOT HAVE THE RESOURCES
CHANGE: I DECIDE AND THE
RESOURCES APPEAR

TANGLE:

I DON'T HAVE RESOURCES

CHANGE:

I DECIDE AND RESOURCES APPEAR

Have you ever wanted something so intensely that you decided to do it at any cost? Do you remember that time? Your intention was total, 100%, you didn't hesitate to do it and had no doubt you could get it. You concentrated on your goal in spite of the fact that you had no idea how you were going to get it. The mechanism was not in your equation. You knew that you needed a mechanism, a way to achieve this, however you were willing to try as many possibilities as needed to get it.

And if you believe you've never been in that situation, we ask you to think again. Go back to your childhood. All children have been in these circumstances at least at some point in their lives. Children are wonderful at getting what they want. They use whatever mechanism they find to get attention even though it is not necessarily a positive one. However, they get the attention. And when the child wants a sweet, a ticket, or to go somewhere, the child does what it takes to get it.

As you get older, you get domesticated and learn to resign, to renounce, to settle, to surrender, to concentrate on the mechanism and not on your wishes. The power of your intention decreases, you feel fear of not being able to achieve your goals, you think you don't deserve it and you stumble and limit yourself to what you can perceive with your five senses. You conform and base your desires on your resources. You stop dreaming. You even start using the word INTENTION in a wrong way, as a weak conditioned desire.

The Larousse dictionary defines the word intention as the determination to do something. Intention is synonymous with purpose, determination and resolution.

Often we hear phrases such as: "had intended to go, but … ", "my intention was to do it, however … " and we complete the sentence with excuses.

When you have the intention, when you decide, you are determined and willing to follow through. The mechanism is something that is secondary. The mechanism is necessary, but not important. There are many ways to arrive at the same place. Only two directions: you are going forward or backward. But you can go in these directions in different ways.

The results are in direct proportion to your intention. Watch your results, and you can assess your true intention.

We are confident that you've heard of athletes, inventors, politicians, religious leaders, actors etc. whose intention was 100% and achieved their goals in spite of their circumstances. When a mechanism does not work, they are looking for another and another without stopping until they reach their goal.

The great Irish playwright, winner of the Nobel Prize for Literature in 1925, and the Oscar in 1838 for the adaptation of a film script, George Bernard Shaw, said: "I do not believe in circumstances, the people who triumph in this world are those who look for the circumstances they want, and if they cannot find them, they make them".

Doña Matilde, an elderly woman, arrived at one of our workshops looking for a ways to succeed in a country where she had just arrived. She heard that the four-day seminar was being held in a couple of weeks and said: "I want to go, but I am "a freeloader with my brother" –she meant she was living with her brother but was not working-. "I have no job and I'm too old". She came back the following week and said virtually the same thing; in the third session, she sharply stated: "I am going to the seminar and I will sell "pupusas" to make money". Pupusas are a version of a Mexican tortilla, generally with meat, cheese and beans, among other ingredients. It is typical food of El Salvador

Doña Matilde sold many pupusas and made great discoveries: that not only did she have a great ability for making the dish, but she was able to socialize, that she was still useful in spite of her age, that she was able to be self-sufficient, that people loved and supported her. After attending the seminar she moved to another city, became independent and began to work on her own.

One of the complaints or excuses that people have is that: "I don't have the means, the circumstances are not in my favor", or that "the plan did not work, there was not the necessary support". Some are very creative with their excuses. They focus on the mechanism, in the form, in the procedure. They do not that their ideas, values and beliefs about themselves and about life limit them and that usually their intention is weak. They do not recognize that it is the fear to fail, to succeed, of the responsibility and many other limiting ideas which prevent them from reaching their dreams.

Clara and Mirna began the partnership although they had no money to buy the equipment or to pay the rent of the premises. However, they did not use this as a reason to set the project aside. They used their skills and few economic resources they had and started the first seminar. They made enough money to acquire the technical equipment (microphones, speakers, computer, etc.). They made a decision, knew what they wanted, and the money came.

If your intention is strong enough you will find your way. Fly without limits. If you feel that you don't have wings, remind yourself that for that reason aircraft were made.

Decide what you really want, have faith and determination.

All I need is 100% intention and the mechanisms will show up.

TANGLE: I AM POOR BUT HAPPY
CHANGE: I AM RICH AND HAPPY

TANGLE:
I'M POOR BUT I'M HAPPY

CHANGE:
I'M HAPPY AND RICH

What is money? It is a tool, is a vehicle. It is energy. Like anything else, money is energy. Money is not the currency that we have. People feel or put their trust in money, but money does not give security. True security is internal; it depends on our faith on God, ourselves and other people.

When you put your trust in money, you give all your power to paper and become a slave to it. Some people feel safe if they have a lot of money. If they don't have it, they become depressed, suicidal, seek divorce, and begin to have a number of problems.

Other people say "money is not important". If you think so, we challenge you to go to the store, ask for food and tell the cashier "I have no money to pay". Then you can come back to say that money is not important. If your son comes and tells you "I am hungry and there is nothing to eat" or "I need the books for school, I want to study" and you don't have the money to cover these needs, can you say again that money is not important?

Of course that is important! It is part of life, we live in a material world and money is a vehicle of exchange in this system. We exchange a service or product for paper. It is as simple as that.

The problem is not the money, but the limiting ideas about money.

Remember that we talked about the subconscious, the autopilot. Let's review the programming or the coordinates that you have about money. Analyzing the ideas that were put in your mental closet about money you can find out where your plane is heading in this area. . Remember the example about the plane that is scheduled to go to Paris when in reality you want to go to Hawaii.

Are you programmed for riches or poverty, for scarcity or abundance?

What are your ideas about money? What did you hear about money while growing up? Do you remember the phrases people around you said when you asked for money? What happened every time your parents talked about money? What happened in your home every time money was the main theme of conversation?

Maybe you heard phrases such as:

- I have no money

- There is no money, or there is not enough

- Money does not grow on trees

- I will buy it tomorrow

- Money attracts money

- Poor but honest

- Money is evil

- Money is dirty

- You have to work hard to make money

- Money does not make you happy

- It is better to be poor, but honest

- It is easier for a camel to go through eye of a needle than for a rich man to get to heaven

- The rich are stingy, and take advantage of the poor

- Money makes you evil

- The rich do not go to heaven

- Money changes people

With a program like this, it is no wonder how poor are results that the majority has in this area. These ideas lead directly to perpetuate poverty.

If you want different results in the financial area, it is essential to change the programming of poverty for one of wealth, shortage for abundance, unworthiness for worthiness, among others.

Let's start analyzing some of the limiting ideas surrounding money.

- There is no money

When someone says this, it is referring to the fact that they do not have the paper that represents money. However if we understand that money is energy and that is created through ideas, it's easy to change the expression to another more productive one. Next time you are tempted to say "there is no money", replace it for "I am going to create the amount I need", "there is enough for everyone and I am learning how to attract it to my life".

- I am poor but honest

This implies that the rich are dishonest, despite the fact that there are many honest millionaires and poor who are dishonest. Honesty has no connection with poverty or wealth. You can be rich and honest at the same time. The money does not make anyone dishonest . Whoever is already dishonest is going to remain that way with or without money. The belief that being rich makes you dishonest, leads to a subconscious fear of being rich, because consciously nobody wants to be dishonest. Finally, you decide to remain poor to avoid becoming dishonest. .

- Money is dirty and evil

"It is the root of all evil" people say, and sometimes they mention the Bible to support their view. If you read the Bible you will realize what it really says is "the love of money is the root of all evil ". Love people and use money, rather than to love money and use people.

Money is neither good nor bad. It is the use that you give it that makes you destroy or build. You can use it to help people or to damage them.

Dave belonged to a company which gave him a bonus of $500,000 dollars. He was a wonderful man with 10 children and a very humble wife. It is important to note that when we're talking about humility, we are not talking about poverty, but humbleness.

He explained that when he lived in a mobile home, there was not enough money to meet the needs of the family, much less to help others, and his mind was usually busy thinking about the money. Now that he had learned how to create it, he could help many, starting with his family. He and his wife go to South America each year to help build schools.

- The rich are stingy and take advantage of the needs of others.

A large number of millionaires donate money to different causes. We have known poor people who are very stingy because they are afraid there is not enough for them and even less to give away. They are convinced that the world owes them and has the responsibility of supplying their needs. They have an entitlement mentality. Also there are poor people who are generous and share what they have. This shows that the generosity or lack of it isn't related to the money itself but to the idea that the person has about money.

- Money does not make you happy

Of course not! Money does not make us happy; it was not designed for that. Money helps us to be comfortable. Happiness is inside you. The truth is that with money we can live more comfortably and can offer comfort to our love ones. When we are happy we attract money easily. If we feel miserable inside, we repel money, we can't think creatively.

Remember that it is through ideas that we create the money. Who is more concerned about money, the people who have money or the ones who don't have it? The ones who don't have it, think about money all the time. The poor man spends a good part of his day concerned about the lack of money, is stressed out thinking: "How am I going to pay my bills, and feed my family? It is never enough, life is unfair, I work and work and I remain poor". Stress leads him to shout, fight and destroy the relations with the people dearest to him. He who has money, and understands the concept of it, focuses on continuing to generate ideas, dedicates his time to create, has the time to read, travel and help others.

Some mention the Bible when they want to prove that the money is bad. "It is easier for a camel passing through the eye of a needle, than to …" We are sure you can finish the sentence with no problem. The conclusion that might be deducted from the sentence is that we must be poor to be able to go to heaven, if we are rich with security then we are going to hell, said the Aristotelian syllogism.

Do you think that in truth that is the meaning of the phrase? We invite you to investigate its origins and its true meaning. The Bible frequently mentions riches as a positive aspect of life. Several passages have been misrepresented because the stories come from the oral tradition and each one is interpreted as the storyteller pleased; so that each person uses a passage according to his own perception, and thus this passage has been perpetuated the notion that poverty is a virtue.

We invite you to keep reviewing the ideas you have about money and decide if they are helping to create abundance or scarcity. In each seminar that we hold, we ask if someone has in his life plan the goal to be poor at the time of retirement. Until today we have not found a single person who says yes. However, the reality is that with the programming held by the majority, the possibilities of becoming financially independent when they reach the age of retirement are minimal. The prevailing coordinates are of scarcity and poverty.

Mr. Antonio was very well known in the town. Every day he pushed his shopping cart and picked up trash, ate debris while his house was falling apart. One day he was found dead in his home and under the mattress discovered a fortune. He had money, but he continued to live as a poor man because he had a poverty mentality. The dream of many is to win the lottery, however, according to the statistics, a large number of winners of the lottery take less than a year to spend all their money and to live worse, financially speaking, than before.

Change your ideas and beliefs about money, modify your coordinates and your results will change.

Let's talk in a practical and simple way of the two basic ways to create money:

1-There is a need, you supply it and you deserve compensation.

This is the basis of every business. This compensation is in direct proportion to the need, the quantity, and the quality with which you supply the need. The need may exist or may be created. For example, you are looking for work as a secretary. You find a company that needs a secretary, you fulfill that need and you get compensated with a salary.

This applies to any job. The same thing happens in businesses, which are based on filling a need and receiving compensation. If someone wants to start a business, he needs to know and look for the needs, or create them, and then find a way to cover them so as to be compensated.

The bigger the need, and the better you meet it, the greater will be your compensation. If there is a need and you supply it only to a small group of people, you're not going to make the same money that you will make if you do it for a large group of people. If you are looking for ways to fill the need of many people, your compensation will multiply.

Here are some of the mind tangles people have about it: a person sees a need, opens a business, and begins to supply the need. The commentary of many is: "he is taking advantage of the need of others".

Ideas create money. Look for a way to fill any need, whether physical, emotional, spiritual or financial and you'll be taking a step to prosper financially.

When the modifications of the mortgages started, some people saw a business opportunity. They sought to meet the need of the people who didn't know how to fill out forms, talk to the bank or the finance company. Some businesses emerged. There was no shortage of comments: "They already are taking advantage of the situation". But the reality is that "they are taking advantage of the opportunity to help others and to generate money". There is the need and there are those who know how to fill it . It is true that some took advantage of the ignorance of the people to steal and deceive. But that is a wrong way to create money. That approach usually does not last very long, or is accompanied by stress and other problems sometimes not necessarily visible to the other.

As long as you follow the universal laws of compensation, it is a fact that you deserve compensation for filling a need. The monetary compensation should be less than or equal to the value provided. When the cost is higher than the value that it is giving, you lose the integrity of the universal laws.

Inevitably you're going to have success if you follow the universal laws.

Imagine that you sell a book to a friend. Your friend asks you how much the book is worth. What he really wants to know is the cost. You charge him $50. He reads the book and finds a phrase that inspires him to change his life positively. How much value has the book then? It depends on the value that your friend gives to his own life. Now, you go to someone else's home and offer that person a book. The lady explains that she does not know how to read and that therefore she cannot see the need to buy the book. You use your selling skills and talk her into buying it. You offer her a great deal. You charge her only $20 dollars for the same book for which your friend paid $50 dollars. The lady places the book on a shelf and leaves it there. She can't read it. The book has no value for her. You had deceived her.

Would you go to the doctor and say " See me for free, because I am sick and you should not take advantage of my illness"? It is true that there are doctors who donate their time, knowledge and service, and do so because their clinics have a sufficient number of patients and income necessary to support people in need.

And what do you think if you go to the store and ask to be given clothing, because it is a necessity and they are taking advantage of your need by charging for the clothes. Likewise, are you expecting your car and home to be free? In our society money is an element of exchange: we give a service or product for money.

For a long time people used to barter, service for service or one product for another product. The system was evolving until gold ingots were the means of exchange for services or products. Today we use paper money which is only a symbol for value.

There is another interesting point. Some employees say: "My boss is becoming rich by taking advantage of me", the employee, in retaliation, arrives late to work. If the entry is at 8:00 a.m. they arrive at 8:05 a.m. and they justify themselves by saying: "The boss does nothing and is becoming rich". They work very slowly and close to the time to finish they stop all the work, because "I don't know what I am doing here", " They are not paying me enough", "I do not like this job".

If you understand that money is energy, think of the energy that you are sending to the universe. By universal law what you send will be returned to you. Some of these employees are dreaming of, one day, becoming business owners. They do not want to receive orders. According to their expectations, these employees hope to be the ones giving the orders and taking advantage of others as their employers are doing.

One day one of these employees starts his own business and very soon discovers that in addition to investing money, now he needs to work not 8 but 12, 14, or even more hours. He realizes that there are employees who have negative ideas of him and his role: His employees think the same thing he had thought of his boss!

In a good number of cases they end up closing the business during the first year. Why does this happen? Did he have bad luck? Absolutely not. The energy was negative; the business was opened for the wrong reasons. If you think of service rather than gain, the compensation will come.

Well now. Let's look at another point. Anyone who starts a business risks time, effort and money to succeed. Usually people see the results, but are not aware of the hours of work, which were necessary to reach that point at which the boss only needs to work a few hours and, in some cases, earn money even when not working. That person, in addition, may be offering jobs and giving the opportunity for those who do not know or do not want to have their own business, those who give a service and are compensated as employees.

Ernesto is a businessman originally from a small village in Oaxaca, Mexico. Thanks to his dedication and commitment he has a company based in Phoenix, AZ where it employs at least 30 employees. Ernesto called Avante Seminar to request training for his employees, because he has full trust in that educating his collaborators his company can expand more and well. Also, he has the goal for making some of his employees managers and for helping them get their own franchises so they become financially independent. AND he is willing to share information in order to achieve this. Ernesto is an enterprising man who trusts his abilities and is convinced that education is the basis for success. Therefore, he invests in his people.

It is likely that some of his employees think that he is crazy, losing time and spending money unnecessarily, because they believe that people do not want to improve their lives. However, Ernesto has worked on his own personal development and has clarity in his objectives. He knows that if you invest in your employees, the gain is multiplied in the financial and emotional areas.

Antonio told us that he had been left without a job because his employer had to close down his company. Antonio recognized that his boss had been very good and generous, even when, due to the economic crisis, he had to make cuts. Several of the employees were angry and began to comment that the boss wanted to "win it all", and that he "was taking advantage of them." Finally the company collapsed and they were left without jobs.

Antonio told us that he always had done everything possible to work in the best way and to understand his boss's situation. A few days later we did see him again. Antonio was happy. His former boss was starting another business and had asked him to work with him, because he was thankful and respected Antonio's work ethic.

Have you ever heard someone complain about the boss where you work all day? And one day, suddenly, seeing that person look sad and depressed having lost the job he/she detested, and where he thought they were taking advantage of him or her.

Usually we suggest that they celebrate. If you get rid of something you don't like, is it not a reason to celebrate?

In the US less than 5% of the population reaches retirement age, 65 years, financially independent. The way of overcoming poverty is not promoting the idea that the other must care for them, or that the money and the rich are bad. We are going to decrease and put an end to poverty when we educate the people and teach them they are worthy, they deserve to be rich.

We change the results by changing the mental awareness programs. The change we must make within ourselves. If you have children, nephews, relatives and friends with scarcity ideas, educate them financially and share this information with them; begin to help in the construction of a different generation, a generation that understands that the world owes them nothing, but they owe the world. With this knowledge we will see a new generation of responsible people with ideas of abundance.

The second idea to create financial abundance is:

2-Give. It is a way to attract money to our lives.

If you want something, give it away. If you want friendship, be a friend. If you want understanding, understand others. If money is what you are looking for, give money. By the universal law, if you give you will receive. It is possible that you don't see the return immediately, however it will happen.

We are going to clarify a few things about giving. When you give, you are sending a message to your subconscious mind that says: "there is plenty, I feel comfortable with the money, I'm grateful".

We said that what is in the subconscious becomes physical reality sooner or later. If in the subconscious there is information of abundance, then the physical result is going to be abundance. The generous person tends to be also very creative. And as we said ideas generate money, and it is not unusual to see that. Contrary to popular belief, rich people tend to be generous. It is not uncommon to hear people say they are going to donate money if they have enough, or when they have some left. Due to a mentality of scarcity, there is never surplus, however. And in this way they are simply reinforcing the ideas of "there is not enough, we don't have enough."

For centuries there has been talk of the tithe. Outside the religious context, the tithe is simply to give 10% of what you earn for the spiritual growth of mankind. There are many ways to help improve the spirituality of the world.

One of the ways to improve our spirituality is through the true education, not only the academic, but the education for life.

Practice the following exercise:

Extend your arms. Close the hands and keep them closed. If someone will give you something when you are in that position, what happens? You can't catch, you can't receive. However, what happens if you open your hand? Can you receive now? Yes, and also you can give!

There is a tendency to close your hand again as soon as you have received and what happens then is that you can't receive more because you are blocking the flow of energy. For giving and receiving it is important to maintain an open position. And this is valid for all areas of our life. Each time you feel that "there is not enough", think of it: you decide if you are going to open or close your hands.

Every time you give, pay attention to your emotions. If you give feeling fearful, insecure, angry, then the message that you send to the subconscious is opposite to what your actions demonstrate.

The language of the subconscious is emotion. It is the emotion which is printed at a deep level. Give with joy, gratitude, and love.

Often we hear people ask if the tithe is calculated before or after taxes. The response that we give them is that they are not ready to give.

It may be that you start giving only 1 %. What is important is the emotion with which you give. The tithe is also payable with community service. In the Latino community, unfortunately, there is not yet the culture of service. As long as we are alive we should be thankful and give back through community service.

One of the experiences of the Leadership Program participants is community service. At the beginning – because they are not used to this idea- community service is perceived as a punishment, as an activity that "has" to be done. However, the change is almost automatic when they realize how easy it is to make a difference in someone's life and in their own. Simple actions, such as carrying bottled water to where they meet people who do not have a home, or spontaneously giving "free hugs", is enough to make a huge impact. Give hugs in public places with signs in English and Spanish, is one of the most rewarding and effective experiences for removing some of the mental tangles. This experience demonstrates that it is children who have no compunction about giving and receiving hugs. Some adults reject them and others are moved from their hearts and come to say: "Thank you, I really needed that, you have made a great difference in my life".

Giving hugs is gratifying. Plus, they are free!

Here, it is worth recalling something that we had already written in previous pages: when we give and in doing so disable someone, you're not giving, you are taking.

Rosa and her children, Marco and Ricardo participated in the four-day seminar. Rosa shared the fact that she had always done everything for them: she cooked, washed and served all the time. In addition she was running a family business and she felt that her children - who were already adults- did not recognize her effort. On the contrary, they waved in her face situations of the past. She believed that her children were ungrateful. She was confused not understanding why her children were resentful with her and her husband.

Rosa realized in a short time, that if you do what the person could achieve by himself, or what he is capable of doing by himself, you are sending the message that you do not have confidence in him and his abilities, and that you, - who are better and know more - have to come to the rescue.

TANGLE: THERE ARE OBSTACLES IN MY WAY
CHANGE: I ALWAYS FIND HELP

TANGLE:

THERE ARE OBSTACLES IN MY WAY

CHANGE:

I ALWAYS FIND HELP

- You are not prepared

- That's for smart people

- You are too slow or too fast

When you express your wishes aloud - perhaps with the hope of finding support – you find yourself with a variety of responses. Each person has a different suggestion. Some examples:

You say: "I want to change my job", "I want to study", "I would like to travel", "I want to marry" or "I want to divorce". And you hear:

- Are you crazy

- You don't have money for that

- There is no time to do that

- You are not good enough

- You are too old or too young

- You have no legal papers

- You are being selfish, you think only on yourself

- You tried before and it did not work

- Be realistic, stop daydreaming, step down from that cloud

- And a many more.

These phrases usually come from those who are closest and, usually, come with good intention. From their hearts they want to protect you, they are afraid you might suffer and speaking from their experiences, they reflect their doubts and fears.

They become your greatest obstacle when you listen to them, and you will sometimes use them as an excuse to not recognize your own fears.

On how many occasions have you said these phrases? How often do you become your own obstacle? Could it be that you do not believe in yourself, have doubts of your skills, are afraid to fail or to succeed, worry about what others might say, or fear to disappoint others?

However, you also find people with a positive mental attitude. They are the ones who say:

- Great idea, you can do it!

- Go ahead, take the chance

- He who does not risk, does not win

- Making mistakes is necessary to learn

- You can find the money

- You can organize your time

- Age is not important if your desire is strong enough

These are the people who support you, encourage you, push you, and believe in you because they trust themselves.

To which of the two groups you listen to?

If you focus on the obstacles, on the reasons for not doing so, on the problem, on the negative, instead of seeing the reasons why you should do it, solutions, what is positive, you're going to finish frustrated, failed, living half way, vegetating, wasting your life to just survive.

Are you an obstacle or a support for those around you? Do you encourage or discourage them? Are you an obstacle or support for yourself?

You were born free, without limits, you did not see any of the obstacles, and you accepted the help and aid of others without conditions. For this reason you reached your goals, you got everything you wanted. When a child starts to walk, for example, he never considers the risk of falling and hurting himself. It does not occur to him that he is not going to be able to do it. The child simply begins little by little to give baby steps, accepts the hand of mom, dad, or of any person who wants to help. And, in a short time, not only does the child walk but he runs.

One day when a boy asks for help and someone answers: " Do it yourself, you don't need anyone else, they don't care about your problems so solve it. You are big enough now!" And little by little you become "the Lone Ranger". Or on the contrary, as the years pass there is always someone to do it for you; they solve all your problems and you become an insecure and dependent person who believes himself unable to do anything. Consequently, you have trouble making decisions because you need someone else's opinion all the time.

Another scenario is that you have been trained to always be helping others while you forget about yourself completely. In that case you are the kind of person who constantly is solving someone else's life while your own life is a disaster. You feel frustrated, alone, misunderstood, used, and you can't say "no". You leave your dreams to one side to live the dreams of others.

Cristina was one of those people who worked too much, catered to all and was left with nothing. She was frustrated because since childhood she was devoted to caring for younger siblings and thus never having time for herself. The pattern continued to repeat while she and her brothers were adults. Cristina realized that she had a huge need for recognition and acceptance, while she helped others to receive affection.

After working intensively on her personal development, Cristina was capable of saying NO with love, without guilt and putting limits. This has not pleased her siblings, who view her as provider of services and money; however, Cristina is satisfied by the achievements and continues working to better herself.

In order to live a balanced life it is important to make an inventory of your strengths and your weaknesses. Traditionally we have been taught to work on our weaknesses to improve our lives. We will give you a different idea: maximizes your skills, and look for ways to compensate for your weaknesses.

As social beings, we need each other. It is a myth that we are completely independent. In reality to be inter-dependent is more healthy and realistic.

Angel is a bright young man and he stated emphatically that "he had succeeded on his own and owed nothing to anybody, because he had scholarships and with that he was getting ahead". In reality he was in a lot of pain because his parents were divorced, and he barely saw his dad. He kept a huge resentment against both. The truth is that Angel received much love and support on the part of his family. He lived in a beautiful house, his mother was a professional and she worked hard to generate enough money for her family. Angel had a car, computer and cell phone for several years. Financially he had no shortcomings - thanks to the efforts of his mother. Emotionally he had large holes and for that reason reassured himself that he needed nobody.

If we analyze the scenario, we can assure you that someone cared for you when were a baby - your parents, grandparents, uncles, godparents or adoptive mothers and fathers. Without them, you would have not survived; someone educated you- even being self-taught, you used the books that someone wrote . If you started to work young, it was because someone gave you work, someone paid you. Someone planted the fruits and vegetables that you eat . Someone made the clothes that you use. If you have a business it depends on what your customers purchase . If you are an employee it is because someone invested time, effort and money to create a company in which you work, etc. We are inter-dependent beings. We need each other and we are definitely connected - not only by the internet - but we have connections at an energy level.

If you use your strengths and associate or make alliances with people who have the skills you don't have, you're going to succeed and be happy. It is a smart way to work.

Learn to ask for support. Don't expect others to guess your thoughts, your desires. Express your needs and wants. Give them the opportunity to support you as you need. And if they are not in a position to help you as you want, respect their decisions and seek help in another place. Be humble, and open to the possibility that the other person can help in different ways. If what you've done so far has not worked, you should try something different. Help and allow others to help you.

It is quite common to see couples, partners or friends who have problems with their differences. The interesting thing is that those differences were the attracting force at one point in their lives, and they can become the catalyst for an extraordinary success.

Marcela is a happy woman, social, at ease with words, extroverted. She loves the holidays . Her husband is quiet, introverted; he enjoys talking with people, but one by one. Marcela wanted him to be as social as she was, and often became frustrated because he did not socialize as she did. The two were working on their personal development. One day, at a party, she was a little upset because he had stayed away from the group and after a while left the room to observe people. It is one of the activities he enjoys.

A young man in the group also went out for a moment and the young man and the husband started to chat. The young man needed to vent and was looking for help. Her husband was that help, the support that the young man needed.

When Marcela heard about it, she began to realize that God uses us in his own way, and that when we accept ourselves and accept others as they are, we can become a great support instead of an obstacle.

Have you ever asked the people close to you, how can I support you? Or do you simply help them as you think they want or as you prefer.

Live life serving, by encouraging and helping others. Grow and help others to grow. Create and facilitate others to believe. Learn and teach. Aid and ask for help. Avoid becoming an obstacle for others and for yourself.

TANGLE: STOP DAYDREAMING
CHANGE: VISUALIZE WHAT YOU WANT

TANGLE:
STOP DAYDREAMING

CHANGE:
VISUALIZE WHAT YOU WANT

When you define what you want in every aspect of your life, it is strongly recommended that you not only write it down, but mold it -depending on your skills - into something tangible and attractive to your eyes. Visualization is a technique through which you can achieve desirable emotional conditions.

This form of mental programming has been used with much success in athletes who want to improve their performance - in addition to the physical practice-.They include visualizations where they see themselves breaking records, going up to the pedestal for first place, achieving extraordinary feats.

That, which you can see with your mind, turns into physical reality. It is therefore important that you visualize what you want to achieve in the four areas of your life: emotional, physical, financial and spiritual.

One of the dynamics that we use to achieve this purpose among the attendees at the seminar is to make a "collage", which in French means "to glue". It is a form of visual art made by the assembly of several forms, images and textures that result in unique and original creations. The materials may be obtained from magazines, newspapers, photographs, colored paper, letters, coins, etc. Anything you can image.

The intention is that you look for images of what you would like to attract into your life, including the emotions: happiness, inner peace, harmony, love, joy, that will take you to get the material goods that you've dreamed of: a beautiful house, a sport car, vacation, money, professional success, a partner, children, healthy food, among others.

If you have thoughts of scarcity, it is time to discard them and allow your imagination to fly through what is called the "Prosperity Map", "Map of abundance" or "My desired future". It is important that the images reflect what you really want. The design has no particular order, there is no sequence and the images don't even have to be linked. Also add your name and positive affirmations such as "I am a leader", "I am intelligent and capable", "I'm sexy", "I am friendly", "I am a good father", "I am a good daughter". Affirmations must always be in present time and in a positive way. Remember that the word " no" is ruled out. The idea is that you see what you want and then you assemble it. You must place your work in a place where you can look at it daily.

A collage helps you orient your goals, makes it easier to define what is important to you; there is no defined path, but when viewing your idea, you know where you want to go. This tool is particularly effective for those who are visual, however to the hearing and kinetic it also helps them focus. If someone wants to add movement to the work, you can place pieces of paper to hang out of the edges of the work so the papers will move with the wind. Be creative, have fun.

When you get your future embodied in the collage, you already know that you must place it in a spot where you can see it every day. One of the participants told us that he had placed his collage in the ceiling of his room, so every morning when he woke up, saw his prosperity map and smiled.

If there is something you haven't added and it suddenly appears in your mind, find a space on your map, give yourself the opportunity to continue growing. This is a work in progress.

The invitation is to start building your future now.

TANGLE: EVERYBODY IS AGAINST ME
CHANGE: I DECIDE MY DESTINY

TANGLE:

EVERYBODY IS AGAINST ME

CAMBIO:

I CHOOSE MY DESTINY

The environment that surrounds you can have a decisive impact on your attitude, but only if you let it.

There are those who get mad when it is hot, and others get sad with cloudy days. We are accustomed to assigning control of our lives to the outside world. If you have money you are happy, if you don't have it you feel unhappy. If you are sick, you get depressed; if you are healthy you don't even notice. The reality is that we don't have control over many of the situations around us —such as the economical deceleration, or climate changes, among others- but we can have control over the attitude with which we face the situations.

Instead of waiting for things to change, it is time to change. Pay attention to that inner voice that says to you: GO AHEAD!, instead of listening to the voices of those who live in conformity and complaining. They are going to continue to do so. However, you decide if you want to listen to them.

You are the only one responsible for your emotions, and if you need help, find it.

One way to begin to make substantial changes in your mood is reviewing your music collection. Yes, as you hear it! Take a look at the songs that you have and the frequency with which you listen to them. If you're the kind of person who has the entire collection of José Alfredo Jiménez and Vicente Fernández, where bitterness, betrayal, pain, and the bottles of alcohol are the main theme, you need to make a musical cleaning. The "narcocorridos" have also found shelter among those who feel identified with the character that, being poor, went on to become "powerful" with real bullets and death. Paquita la del Barrio is a wonderful woman who with her songs has given voice to many women who resented their spouses.

On one occasion, while we had a workshop, the daughter of one of the participants was waiting in the adjoining room and was entertained by listening to music through earphones. Suddenly the meeting was interrupted because the girl started singing very loud: "vermin, poisonous snake, garbage, I hate you, rat of two legs I'm speaking to you ..."

The mom apologized for the interruption, which gave us the opportunity to talk about the content in the media which are stored in the subconscious. The girl, barely nine years old, was listening to the songs that her mom had at home. For her, the lyrics did not make any sense, perhaps she might not even have understood them, because she spoke more English than Spanish; however the ideas of defiance, treason, insults and revenge were already planted through a song. The same is true with soap operas where the anti-core values are common: hatred, revenge, betrayal, guilt, punishment and resentment. It is commonplace to witness scenes in which there are blows, insults, ill-treatment and multiple acts of domestic violence, where the men beat and shout at their spouses.

Estela had spent time in a shelter for women who have suffered domestic violence, and commented that she had not even realized that she was a victim, until one day while reading an article in the newspaper, she became aware of the symptoms of domestic violence. She discovered that were not only physical beatings, but psychological as well as emotional manipulation and financial control. Estela recalled that in her house her father beat and yelled at her mother, and kept her short of money so she did "not get out of control". Estela was married to a man just like her dad, whose behavior she thought was normal. What is extraordinary is that she shared the fact that she used to watch soap operas, where in many scenes the men took advantage of women, either with physical and/or verbal violence. "I believed that was normal, because it was on TV" said Estela.

The message that is being sent at the subconscious level is that violence is normal. In the house there was yelling, hitting, throwing things and deceiving just like in the soap operas which people believe are a reflection of reality. That is what girls and boys learn through the television dramas. Add to that the wide range of information that is obtained over the internet and through video games.

Make a review of what your mind and your children's mind are storing.

You can to decide to make substantial changes by choosing music that encourages you to be better person, to getting ahead, to achieving your dreams. In the music market there are plenty of self-help themes; there are internationally known singers and composers who share their ideas for a better world. In addition, instead of investing hours and hours in front of the TV, computer or handheld video games, you can go for a walk, exercise or talk with your children and your partner. Turn off all electronic devices while you are together. Of course, that means the cell phone too! Listen and watch materials with edifying content which speak of progress, harmony and peace, instead of treason, cowardice and murders.

Play rewarding music, or read some pages of a motivational and human development books when you feel "down". There are also audio - books, to deal with the excuse that you don't like reading.

The only one responsible for your mood, is you. Help yourself; you're your best doctor and psychologist!

OR you can continue to blame others for your results, join the club of "ACUTE VICTIMITIS", point fingers, judge, criticize and justify the mediocrity.

The best creation of mankind is reading this book, so you're able to make changes in your thinking, your feelings and therefore in your results. These changes may seem insignificant, however major changes are achieved with small actions and one at a time.

If you have ever heard the phrase: "You are the architect of your own destiny", pay attention, it is true.

Don't forget that you are solely responsible for your results. You can reprogram your mind to fail or succeed.

TANGLE: LIFE IS A DRAMA
CHANGE: LIFE IS LEARNING FROM THE DRAMA

TANGLE:
LIFE IS A DRAMA

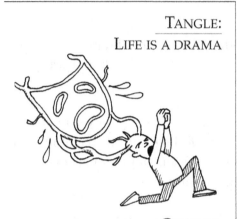

CHANGE:
LIFE IS LEARNING FROM THE DRAMA

In this book we wanted to capture the teachings and lessons of the seminar THE CHALLENGE OF CHANGING YOUR LIFE, an intense program of four days duration where participants are given the opportunity to see what works and does not work in order to start making changes.

However, it is not a precise document of the issues and processes. There are many dynamics in the program that we have ruled out in this text because we must implement them in order to understand them.

Also during the process emotions come up and to describe them in a book is not possible. Our goal is to give you tools so you can begin to look within yourself. The goal is to make the first changes through the reading of this material. The invitation is for you, very soon to decide to make substantial changes by participating in the seminar.

What we'll do then is to share with you some of the moments when people realized how they could begin to make changes through reinterpretation of the facts. As we said earlier, the facts have already passed and you are not going to be able to change them, they are part of the past. What it is possible to do is to change the interpretations to ones that give you inner peace.

Here some examples where X is the participant and A is Avante:

X - Usually I do not express my feelings when I am in any situation, even knowing the answer, I do not reply.

A - Why don't you express your feelings?

X - I am afraid, it always happens that way. That's the way I have always lived. Many times I want to say something, and I do not have the courage to say it or do it. I am afraid to make a mistake and have people get upset with me

A - When did you start being afraid?

X - I have always being fearful.

A - I assure you that when you were a baby you were not afraid. When you were three, four or five years old you were bold and courageous and did not think of the consequences, that is what children do: they do it with no fear. When did you start being fearful?

X - I am adopted. I did not know my dad. I see my parents –the ones who raised me- as my parents. My dad never beat me, but my mom was stricter.

A - When did you find out you were adopted?

X - Since I can remember.

A - Remember what you felt when you understood what being adopted meant?

X - I asked myself, why did they do that? Why did they not keep me? Did I do something wrong? Why did they not love me? In my teen days I met my biological mom, I felt she did not care about me, since she spoke with me only three times.

A - What do you feel when you remember your biological parents abandoned you?

X - I feel sad and scared. I thought maybe I did something wrong, and I was afraid my parents, the ones who raised me, could abandon me, too. Frequently I asked myself, what if they don't love me anymore like my biological parents did.

A - The five year old is making decisions. Which decisions did you make?

X - I wanted to do everything right and be quiet so they would love me. I preferred not to talk so they wouldn't get upset with me because I did not want them to abandon me.

A - Did you think that if you stayed quiet, in silence, being a good boy, they would love you? Because, according to your interpretation, you had done something wrong for your biological parents not to love you. Let's analyze this as an adult, since you are not a kid anymore. Was it your fault that your parents decided to give you away? Is it possible to blame a little kid for this?

X - No, of course not. However, that was what I thought.

A – Let's re-interpret this episode of your life. Is it possible your mom gave you away because she loved you so much, she wanted to give you an opportunity with the other family? She gave you the opportunity to have a home and the things a little kid needed to grow up healthy according to her. Is it possible that instead of "not loving you" she "loved you a lot", she had the courage to let you go and give you away thinking you were going to be better off?

X - Yes, it is possible. I never thought it that way, since it was too painful just to think she abandoned me. I think she was a teenager when she got pregnant with me.

A - So she was just a teenager when she became a mom! Can you image her fear of the responsibility of becoming a mom? Additionally, you need to consider the fact that our society judges heavily a single pregnant woman. Can you understand the emotional burden?

X - I am sure she wanted for me something better than what she could offer

A - Looking at it from another point of view, since the moment you were born you have been a loved child, one who has done nothing wrong, who has the right and deserves to be happy; who does not need to allow abuse or to remain silent to be loved. A child can make mistakes, get ahead in life, and he will always be loved. So, what are you going to do differently?

X - Fist of all, I am going to have the courage to do the things I want to do, in spite of fear, because I am able. Now I understand my fears are old since I was attached to the idea that being adopted meant I had no right to speak.

In early childhood when interpretations of the events that occur and decisions based on them are made, these interpretations are usually about yourself and your value as a person. The goal is to protect you from pain or to be loved.

The child tends to think everything that happens like overprotection, domestic violence, alcoholism, sexual abuse, fights, his parents' discussions, or a reprimand is his fault. The child feels that he did something wrong, that there is something wrong with him, people do not want or love him, that they have abandoned him, or rejected him, and that he has to fulfill the expectations of the parents to be loved and accepted. These and many other deductions pass through his head, based on his short experience. Based on this, he will make decisions that will control his life. For example, the child may decide that it is better to be quiet to avoid problems, thinking that in this way people will love him. He will live his life in in silence allowing others to abuse him or her, with the hope of being accepted and loved. They are great candidates to live in abusive relationships.

Others, on the contrary, decide they are not going to let anyone take advantage of them and become aggressive; they are always on the defensive. It is a way of protecting themselves. We see them all the time upset, frowning, keeping others away so as not to be hurt. Internally they are angry, but also sad, because at the end of the day a sad person keeps a lot of resentment and anger, and an angry person has a profound sadness; they are just disguising it.

There are those who decide to protect themselves through jokes and an "I don't care" attitude. In schools, these children are generally friendly, talk a lot and when they grow up they keep doing the same. They do not talk about their problems, they pretend to not feel and they put on a mask of happiness. They used the mechanism of "forgetting" the past as a form of protection.

In a simplistic way, this is the explanation of how we act. We are carrying the emotions of the five year old child and, according to the experts we become addicted to those emotions.

If you can discover to which emotion you are addicted, you've taken a great step toward your healing.

Another participant speaks:

X - Usually I do not pay attention to what I do and I get very angry when I feel I can't do something. I get desperate with everybody and yell at them. I do not like to be in the front, and I criticize everyone and everything. I always let others do what I can do and I scream too much, my wife says.

A - Why do you yell?

X - I get frustrated. I yell at my kids because it is the only way they listen.

A - They are used to it, you conditioned them. Why so much frustration? Look back, that emotion must come from some situation of the past. What happened?

X - I was the youngest and I remember my dad used to come home drunk and beat my brothers and my mom. He did not hit me, maybe because I was the baby.

A - What do you feel when you remember those events?

X - I feel powerless, angry, with a desire to scream, but I can't because I am afraid.

A - Against whom do you feel anger?

X - My dad. I can't understand why he beat up my mom. Also I am angry at my brothers because they did not defend themselves and my mom.

A - I am talking with the little kid, are you upset with your mom?

X - My mother suffered a lot. However, thinking twice, I was angry at her because she allowed it. Sometimes I wanted to be big to kill my dad and free my mom. One day I faced him and my mom intervened and defended him. I was so angry!

A - What happened?

X - My father did nothing to me. But I remember he hit my brothers and I felt guilty. If I had not faced my dad, things would have calmed down.

A- What did you decide to do?

X - I thought it was better to remain quiet, because when I spoke up everything got complicated. I did not want my mother and brother to suffer and then they would not love me. Before when I had been quiet and hide, things were not so bad. However, every time I remain in silence I feel a horrible pressure in my chest and I end up yelling.

A- And you still doing it.

X - Yes, I know. I promised myself I will never hit someone weaker than me, and sometimes I really want to hit somebody so I prefer to shout. In other occasions what I really want to do is to cry.

A - Do you cry?

X - Of course not! I don't want to be seen crying, they are going to think I am stupid, weak, gay.

A - And if you shout?

X - The kids obey, and everybody else stays away from me. If they are far away I can no longer hurt them. The truth is that I'm angry with myself for being such a coward.

A - Why do you say you are a coward?

X - Because I never defended my mom again. The truth is that I was afraid.

A - How old were you?

X - About six years old.

A - Let's re-interpret this situation. You think a six year old child may face an adult without getting hurt? .

X - No. My dad is big and strong. If my older brothers and my mom could not deal with him, how could I?

A - So are you really a coward? Or did you just behave like a kid your age? And about your parents, what do you know about their lives?

X - My father was beat up by his dad frequently and by his mom too. I remember he commented that he did not have a childhood and that he started to work at an early age. About my mom, she was the youngest and there was domestic violence in her home.

A - Do you begin to understand that they gave you what they had and they did the best they could? Like many people they were repeating the family story, just as you are doing it right now. How do you think your children feel when you yell at them?

X - Fearful. It hurts to admit it, however now I understand they obey me due to fear not respect. I know they feel it. I felt that fear for a long time and I still feel it every time I am in a situation I can't handle. I suppose my wife is also afraid of me

A - It would be good for you to talk with her and ask.

X - I'll do it. And above all I want to work to let go of the fear and anger.

A - You just made a huge step to moving toward the process of forgiveness. Now you understand and are willing to let go, you are ready to forgive.

There is no way to change the facts; however we can change our interpretation of them. To remember our past and to evaluate the interpretations that we made of the different facts that we live, is one of the steps to forgiveness, and when we forgive we are liberated. We can always re-interpret the events, if we want.

Someone asked us, during a seminar, if this was not a way to deceive ourselves. Definitely this is not a deception. We are not denying what happened, we are only seeking to understand and in this way find the learning, the gift. However, as the subconscious mind believes everything that we say to it, it is a matter of deciding what we want to believe. Do you prefer to believe you are worthless, don't deserve anything because your parents left you, beat you up, or someone abused you mentally, physically or sexually? Or would it work better for you to understand that each person does the best with what she/he has and gives only what she/he has; that their behavior has nothing to do with you and your value? You decide.

Some people ask: is it possible to change during a weekend? The answer is yes. Now for the changes to become permanent it is important to continue working on yourself daily. The changes won't happen magically, it takes time and effort, and in some cases money. Sometimes we need professional help to re-interpret the events.

We are spiritual beings having physical experiences, and we have a mind. Why then do we dedicate more time to the physical than the emotional and spiritual areas? You eat and take a shower daily. What would happen if you didn't shower? You guessed it! The same will happen with your emotional and spiritual areas, if you don't take care of them daily. If you neglect them, just for a few days, they will stink!

TANGLE: GOD IS GOING TO PUNISH YOU
CHANGE: GOD LOVES YOU

TANGLE:
GOD IS GOING TO PUNISH YOU

CHANGE:
GOD LOVES YOU

We are born with guilt stuck to our backs; we grow with guilt and easily learn to blame others for everything that happens to us.

The burden of guilt is enormous, beginning with the ideas of original sin that have been transmitted by generations without questioning.

We learn to feel guilty for fear of punishment: if we sin we go straight to hell, where we "will burn" for the violations. We are told that.

Ever since we were children we are taught that if we do something wrong or incorrectly, -according to adults - "God will get really get mad with us and He will punish us.

We need to understand that God, Superior Energy, Mahomet, Jehovah, Buddha, or whatever you want to call what nourishes our spirit to connect our soul to the higher source, a source of creation and love Our God or gods do not need to have an inquisitor eyes to view the actions of each person because we are endowed with conscience . It is when we know this that we can stop fearing Him and begin to love and respect Him. The only emotion we should feel toward Him is LOVE.

The opposite of LOVE is FEAR. Everything else comes from that. Control is maintained through fear tactics; fear is used to manipulate and control people and the masses. Fear and fear of punishment drive people to stop living with intensity. Those chains of guilt are transmitted from generation to generation.

When we see God as a loving source which expects us to awake to the reality of His love so that we can return home, then we are liberated and can be happy.

We are liberated in order to love God, love ourselves and love our brothers. We can stop judging because we understand that God does not judge.

We learn to forgive when we understand that we need forgiveness, too, when we believe that someone has hurt us or that we have hurt someone. We also understand that God does not forgive because He does not judge. We are made in the image and likeness of the creator, so we're perfect. We are spiritual beings. Our spirit is perfect because it is God's creation. You can call it a different name, however in all civilizations there has been a belief in a higher power, a creative source that allows us to be thankful.

Some choose to believe in God to be thankful for everything which is received, otherwise we would not know who to thank. It is not necessary to be religious to have faith. You can be religious without being spiritual, and spiritual without a religion.

God is only love, and God wants us to be happy. God does not ask anything from us, He expects nothing except that we love Him so that we can love ourselves.

God loves you. God does not call for sacrifices, suffering, or pain on your part. He is not waiting for you to make a mistake to punish you. He only wants for you to awaken from this dream of madness and understand that He is love. And, forgiveness is the means by which we can understand and experience His love.

How can you say you love God while you criticize, judge, blame, envy, hate your brother? How can you preach the love of God while practicing the hatred and resentment toward yourself and others?

How do you talk about having faith in God and not trust yourself?

Is it possible to love God and hate your brother? How can you say you love God while discriminating against His children based on the color of their skin, religion, political affiliation, ideas, sexual preferences, etc.?

Do you feel superior to your brother, while forgetting that you both are God's creation? Or do you think you are less than others, ignoring your divinity?

You believe that to accept your greatness is prepotency, and waste your talents. Then you blame God for your results.

It is time to accept your greatness, because it comes from God. It is time to shine and to allow God to use you. It is time to be happy and to love God as He loves us. Forgive, be happy, love unconditionally. Feel God's love and be thankful. Accept yourself and your brother. We are one with the Creator. Let us walk together back home, back to our Creator.

TANGLE: I WILL START TOMORROW
CHANGE: I START NOW

TANGLE:

I WILL START TOMORROW

CHANGE:

I START RIGHT NOW

Image an hourglass. If the sand represents your life, then the sand in the bottom is your past and the grains of sand in the top are your future. Now, if you observe carefully, you will notice that in the middle of the glass the sand keeps moving constantly. The sand on the top comes down without stopping. That's our life.

A large number of people keep their attention on what is in the bottom, what is in the past. They constantly lament what could or should have been done. These people relive over and over again what happened and again feel the pain, fear, anger. Meanwhile, others are concentrated in the sand above, in the future. These people always are concerned about what might happen, unsure of tomorrow. And in the meantime, the sand is still moving, life continues to make progress, and they do not notice.

Do you know how much sand is on the top part of your hourglass? Do you know how much life you have left?

The truth is that we do not know. Some think they have a lot when in reality have just a little bit. Others, on the contrary, live convinced they don't have too much left and then live many years.

Clara's dad died suddenly. He was only 52 years old. "The doctors found an aneurysm and his life ended there. The interesting thing is that we thought he had a lot of sand left on his hourglass. Her granddad died at the age of 80, so she believed her dad was going to last that long. His life was shorter than she imaged. The same happen to her mother in law who died at 48 of a heart attack. She remembered her dad lived each day with intensity; he did not worry about tomorrow and was always ready to help a friend, to serve. He smiled frequently. When talking about the past he was cheerful and emphasized the learning from each experience. He had no idea how much sand was left, but lived as he had only a grain of sand".

Clara commented, "I heard a friend saying that he is going to die soon, that his days are counted. In fact, he has been saying that for a long time. He thinks there is little sand and in truth it seems that there is plenty".

How do you live? Do you live as if you have a lot of sand or a little? Do you procrastinate? Why do you live your life as if you had an eternity? Why do you live with the certainty of tomorrow?

Tomorrow I will start school, tomorrow I will tell that person I love him, tomorrow I will reconcile with my friend, my brother, my dad or my mom, tomorrow I will hug my children, tomorrow I will let them know how much I love them.

Who told you there is something more than NOW, THIS moment?

Who assured you that you are going to have a tomorrow?

However, you want to keep living your life for tomorrow: tomorrow I will change jobs; tomorrow I will stop doing this; tomorrow I will stop smoking; tomorrow I will stop drinking; tomorrow I will enjoy my kids, tomorrow. I am going to dedicate time to my family, tomorrow; I will start the diet, tomorrow; I will begin to take care of myself, tomorrow; I will go to the doctor, tomorrow. Tomorrow I will begin to love myself.

The reality is that tomorrow does not exist. The only thing is NOW! This is the moment; this is the only thing you have, NOW! The truth is that you have no idea how much sand there is on the top part of your hourglass. And the sand that has already fallen there is no way to put it up. The past was. We learn from it, however we cannot change it.

When will you begin to live with intensity?

When are you going to start looking at things in a different way?

When are you going to re-interpret your past to live a different present?

Now it is the time to hug your spouse!

Now it is the time to tell her you love her! Now it is the time to tell you kids how much you love them!

Now it is the time to love them and let them know how important they are in your life! Now is the time to help your friend!

Tomorrow it is possible that they won't need you, because maybe they won't be here.

This is the moment to focus on the middle part of your hourglass. The sand keeps moving without stopping, today, now. Even if you concentrate on yesterday or on tomorrow, the present is the only real thing. Now it is the time to start studying!

Now it is the time to reach your dreams!

Now it is the time to be thankful!

Now it is the time to do something for your life!

Now it is the time to make decisions!

Now it is the time to change! Now it is the time to live!

It's never late to start.

Tomorrow does not exist. Nobody guarantees tomorrow, nobody guarantees that this people are going to be with us tomorrow..

Who ensures you that your children are going to be with you tomorrow?

Who ensures you that your friend is going to need you tomorrow?

Who ensures you that you're going to have health tomorrow?

Now is the only thing you have.

What if you start living your life now, at this precise moment?

What if you decide to change your life now, at this very moment?

What if you start taking risk now?

What if you start making mistakes now?

What if you start learning now?

What if you remember that today is all you have?

Live plentifully today!

Live in excellence today!

Give 100% today!

Be happy today!

Forgive today!

Let go today!

Love today!

Shine today!

Be light today!

Illuminate others' path today!

Do something different today!

Develop your potential today!

Be thankful because you are alive today, this moment!

Leave tomorrow to God.

Today is the first day of the last day of your life.

Printed in the United States
By Bookmasters